KNEELING IN THE END ZONE

KNEELING IN THE END ZONE

SPIRITUAL LESSONS FROM THE WORLD OF SPORTS

JOSH TINLEY

THE PILGRIM PRESS
CLEVELAND

FOR

Ashlee, Meyer, Resha Kate, and Malachi

The Pilgrim Press, 700 Prospect Avenue, Cleveland, Ohio 44115
thepilgrimpress.com
© 2009 by Josh Tinley

Printed in the United States of America on acid-free paper

13   12   11   10   09   5   4   3   2

Library of Congress Cataloging-in-Publication Data

Tinley, Josh.
    Kneeling in the end zone : spiritual lessons from the world of sports / Josh Tinley.
        p. cm.
    Includes bibliographical references.
    ISBN 978-0-8298-1842-0 (alk. paper)
    1. Sports—Religious aspects.   2. Sports—Moral and ethical aspects.
3. Athletes—Religious life.   4. Spirituality.   I. Title.
GV706.42.T56 2009
248.8'8—dc22   2009002986

CONTENTS

Acknowledgments

———

Foremost, I must thank my wife Ashlee and my children Meyer, Resha Kate, and Malachi for their patience with me as I wrote this book. I am especially grateful to Ashlee—who allowed me to spend several afternoons hiding out in coffee shops and restaurants with a laptop, a Bible, and a copy of Bill Russell's autobiography—and Malachi, who was born while I was working on this project. (For that matter, I should thank the Women's Hospital at the Centennial Medical Center in Nashville for providing wireless Internet access on their labor and delivery floor.)

I owe a debt of gratitude to my father, who took me to see so many basketball games and other sporting events when I was young; to my mother, who drove me to countless practices during my childhood and youth; to both of my parents, who gave me opportunities to try my hand at several sports, many of which I was not terribly good at; and to my sister, whose weekly conversations with me about sports have been invaluable to the content of this book.

I am grateful to all the editors and publications that have been willing to publish my work, especially Liz Garrigan with the *Nashville Scene* and Will Penner and Tim Baker with the *Journal of Student Ministries*. Special thanks are in order for my employer, The United Methodist Publishing House, for allowing me to explore connections between faith and culture as a writer and editor, and for my Sunday school class at Belmont United Methodist Church in Nashville, for participating in the lessons I put together each week.

I appreciate the help of my former college roommate, Dennis Goodman, who helped me more fully understand that plight of Cubs fans, and of the athletic department at Immaculata University, which granted me interviews with former players and fans of the great Immaculata Mighty Macs championship teams from the 1970s.

Finally, I must thank The Pilgrim Press and editor Kim Martin Sadler for giving me the opportunity to write this book. This book has given me an occasion to remember my own (admittedly unimpressive) athletic exploits. I hope that this book honors the memories of my high school swimming coaches, Jan Hendricks and Brian Councilman, whose strict practice regimens I discuss in chapter 6.

INTRODUCTION

First things first. I have to give thanks to my
Lord and Savior up above. THANK YOU, JESUS!

—FORMER RAMS QUARTERBACK KURT WARNER
celebrating his team's victory in Super Bowl XXXIV

Do you not know that in a race the runners all compete,
but only one receives the prize? Run in such a way that you may
win it. Athletes exercise self-control in all things; they do it to
receive a perishable wreath, but we an imperishable one.
So I do not run aimlessly, nor do I box as though beating the air;
but I punish my body and enslave it, so that after proclaiming
to others I myself should not be disqualified.

—1 CORINTHIANS 9:24–27

JUMBOTRON EVANGELISM

Few Americans today would recognize the name Rollen Stewart, but
between 1977 and 1992, "Rockin' Rollen" was one of the most recognizable personalities in American sports. In the late seventies, Stewart,
donning a rainbow afro wig, frequently attended nationally televised

sporting events and made sure that the cameras would find him waving his arms and wearing a toothy grin. His appearances were carefully orchestrated and motivated by a desire for fame and fortune. Stewart's "Rainbow Man" character made him a minor celebrity and even garnered him a brief endorsement deal with Budweiser that covered his living and travel expenses for two years.

What began as a publicity stunt and get-rich-quick scheme became a means of evangelism when Stewart found Christ following the 1980 Super Bowl. His lust for notoriety had left him feeling empty and depressed, and after watching televangelist Charles Taylor in his hotel room Stewart decided that he needed to live for something greater than himself. He sold all of his assets and decided to no longer "prostitute" himself with endorsement deals. He lived in his car and bathed at rest stops. Soon thereafter, the rainbow wig was always accompanied by a sign reading "John 3:16." John 3:16, of course, is arguably the best known verse in the Bible, a concise explanation of God's plan of salvation through Christ: "For God so loved the world that he gave his only Son, so that everyone who believes in him may not perish but may have eternal life." For Stewart, televised sporting events made an ideal venue for answering Jesus's Great Commission: "Go therefore and make disciples of all nations" (Matt. 28:19a).

Stewart spent the 1980s doing JumboTron evangelism and subsisting on donations. His donors shelled out enough cash to send the Rainbow Man to several World Series, Super Bowls, NBA Finals, Stanley Cup Finals, Indy 500s, college championships, and Olympic Games. The 1986 FIFA World Cup (soccer) in Mexico gave Stewart the opportunity to get his wig and favorite scripture in front of hundreds of millions (possibly billions) of television spectators worldwide. After a while, the rainbow wig disappeared and the focus shifted entirely to John 3:16.

Before long, stadium officials and sports broadcasters grew tired of Stewart's antics. He had to work harder to get on television because camera operators tried to avoid getting him in the shot. NBC golf producer Larry Cirillo allegedly threatened to hire someone to break Stewart's legs if he didn't stop holding up the sign. Stewart's wife, who'd been living with him in their car, left him after he allegedly choked her during an argument about sign placement. Eventually,

Stewart's money ran out, his car was totaled by a drunk driver, and he was homeless on the streets of Los Angeles.

For years, Stewart had sensed that the end was near. And, as Stewart faced rejection from television producers, his message of salvation took on an eschatological character, warning people that the end of the world was imminent. To draw attention to doomsday prophets and end-times preachers, Stewart fashioned himself as the antichrist. Holding up signs gave way to stink-bomb attacks; among his targets were a church, a newspaper office, and a Christian bookstore. Instead of wearing a rainbow wig to get attention, he wrote letters laced with apocalyptic language that included hit lists of pastors.

The Rainbow Man made his last stand in a Los Angeles airport hotel in September 1992. Convinced that the world would end in days (and that Juan Carlos of Spain would be revealed as the Beast in Revelation), he planned to kidnap and hold for ransom two day laborers he'd picked up while posing as a contractor. The workers escaped when Stewart drew a gun, but a chambermaid who'd been in the room when the men arrived was stuck as Stewart's hostage. Undeterred, the disturbed former celebrity demanded a three-hour press conference so that he could preach his message to the world. Law enforcement did not comply. Instead, they used a concussion grenade to knock Stewart unconscious and took the Rainbow Man to jail. Stewart is currently serving three life sentences.

Prior to Rollen Stewart's descent, any casual sports fan would have recognized the Rainbow Man. And copycats continue holding up "John 3:16" signs at sporting events, albeit often without the wig. There is no way to measure the fruits of the efforts of Stewart and his lesser known counterparts. We cannot know how many spectators have dusted off their family Bibles and turned to the third chapter of the fourth Gospel, nor can we know how many of these people took to heart Christ's message of salvation. We do know that Stewart and those whom he inspired felt a connection between or a need to connect faith and athletics.[1]

THANK YOU, JESUS!

During the 1999–2000 sports year, I lived in Evansville, Indiana, about halfway between my native Indianapolis and Nashville, where I now re-side. Evansville was where I began the geographic and emotional transition from being an Indianapolis Colts fan to being a Tennessee Titans fan. Both teams had finished the 1999 season 13–3. The Colts made the playoffs as winners of the AFC's East division, the Titans as the AFC's top wild card. Tennessee opened the playoffs at home against Buffalo, a game that ended with the legendary (at least here in Nashville) Music City Miracle. This miracle did not involve a suspension of the laws of nature, only an unlikely lateral from tight end Frank Wycheck to receiver Kevin Dyson in the game's closing seconds.

The following week, the Titans met the Colts in the RCA Dome in Indianapolis. Although the teams had identical records, the Colts—with home field advantage and the triple threat of Peyton Manning, Marvin Harrison, and Edgerrin James—were favored. At the time, my heart was much closer to Indy than Tennessee, so I was disappointed when the Titans pulled the upset, knocking the Colts out of the playoffs. But with the Colts out of the mix, I decided that the Titans were my favorite of the remaining playoff teams. I was glad to see Tennessee continue its run, defeating top-seeded Jacksonville for the third time that season to advance to the Super Bowl.

In the big game, Tennessee faced the St. Louis Rams, who were led by league MVP Kurt Warner. The Rams signed Warner as a backup, but he got the starting job when first-string quarterback Trent Green suffered a preseason injury. Warner's story was extraordinary. He was not drafted out of college and had spent time in the Arena Football League and NFL Europe—along with a stint stocking shelves at an Iowa grocery store—before making an NFL roster. Warner didn't just manage the offense in Green's absence. He put together one of the best seasons by a quarterback in league history: 4,353 yards, forty-one touchdowns, and a 65.1 completion percentage.

Sadly, the Titans finished Super Bowl XXXIV one yard short of sending the game into overtime. Warner passed for 414 yards, a Super Bowl record, and threw a seventy-three-yard touchdown pass to Isaac Bruce that gave the Rams the lead with just over two minutes remaining. During the postgame celebration, the broadcast team handed Warner, the game's MVP, the microphone. "First things first," Warner told the crowd in Atlanta and the millions watching on television. "I have to give thanks to my Lord and Savior up above. THANK YOU, JESUS!"[2]

To be entirely honest, I have to admit that Warner's inspirational grocery-clerk-to-Super-Bowl-MVP story gave me chills. But while I could appreciate his faith and his perseverance, I took exception to Warner's crediting Jesus for his Super Bowl win. I suppose one could argue that God willed the Rams to victory so that Kurt Warner's story of transformation and perseverance could inspire some of the millions of Super Bowl viewers to accomplish seemingly impossible feats for the glory of God. But as someone who hoped that the Titans would win Super Bowl XXXIV (and one who has become much more of a Titans fan in the seasons that have followed), I cannot accept that God was somehow working against my team. The thought of Christ wearing a Kurt Warner #13 Rams jersey, thrusting a blue-and-gold foam finger as Warner completed his now famous seventy-three-yard touchdown pass to Isaac Bruce, seems absurd, as does the notion that the deity would cheer with "pep and vim" (to quote my alma mater's fight song[3]) for any team or player.

That said, no person of faith would claim that God is not present when athletes compete on the court, field, or track, or in the pool. But how is God present? In what ways is God revealed through sports?

BAPTIZING SPORTS

Rockin' Rollen and Kurt Warner are just two of many athletes, coaches, fans, or broadcasters who have found ways to inject God and their faith into the world of sports. Several football players kneel in the end zone to say a quick prayer after scoring a touchdown (although doing so in an NFL game may result in a fifteen-yard penalty for excessive celebration). Broadcasters often invoke the biblical story of David and Goliath to describe the chances of an underdog prevailing in a lopsided matchup. The outcomes of sporting events on Saturday are the subjects of thanks at worship on Sunday morning, while Sunday's games are the object of pregame petitions. Players and coaches in all sports praise God for their successes and ask God for the strength to endure their struggles.

This book takes the opposite approach to the relationship between faith and sports. Rather than looking for ways that God is involved (or can be involved) in sports, it looks at stories from the world of sports that are themselves reflections of the divine. What can Cubs fans teach us about hope? What can we learn about being one in Christ from Joe Louis, Roberto Clemente, and Billie Jean King? What lessons about faith and perseverance can we glean from George Mason University's unlikely run to the Final Four in 2006? This book explores ways in which sports illustrate essential principles such as perseverance, humility, and redemption. It also uses sports in metaphors, drawing parallels between scriptural stories and memorable tales from the field and court. As you can see in the epigraph at the beginning of this introduction, the Apostle Paul employed a similar tactic, using sports metaphors to teach his readers in Corinth about discipline, perseverance, and self-control.

Basketball great Bill Russell said that sports are one of the "Big Four." "Only four kinds of events—politics, religion, the arts, and sports—have been able to draw consistently large crowds of paying customers throughout history," he says. "That must mean something."[4]

It must. People care about sports. Sports are an obsession for many and an idol for some. People order their lives around games and tournaments. They invest large sums of money in tickets and paraphernalia, and in some cases have been known to help their alma mater pay millions of dollars in penalties to get rid of an underperforming coach before his contract is up. They allow the outcomes of competitions to determine whether they are happy, distressed, relieved, anxious, or angry.

While this book addresses the dangers of sports obsession and idolatry, its larger purpose is to acknowledge the love that people—including people of faith (and particularly Christians)—have for games and competitions and to give them a way to "baptize" the sports they care about so much. My hope is that readers will begin to see glimpses of God in the sports they watch and to learn something from their favorite athletes about how to live as children of God and disciples of Christ.

1

"LIFE BEGINS ON OPENING DAY"

Hope amid Wilderness and Exile

I literally watch parts of 145–150 [Cubs] games a year.
At this point in my life, I would not know how to turn that off.
And once the passion is there, of course you hope they win. . . .
They will win it again at one point; I might as well
be there when it happens.

—CUBS FAN DENNIS GOODMAN

For thus says the Lord of hosts,
the God of Israel: Houses and fields and vineyards
shall again be bought in this land.

—JEREMIAH 32:15

———

Randy Horick, former sports columnist for the *Nashville Scene* and a member of West Nashville United Methodist Church in Nashville, recalls an annual ritual in his congregation:

Every February for the past 15 years, . . . [during] the time of the worship service when members offer their joys and concerns, Dave Hormby would raise his hand, indicating that his wife,

Kathie, had something to offer. In February, everyone knew what Kathie would say. They'd wait quietly for 30 seconds or more until they heard a slightly metallic female voice from Kathie's laptop computer: "Pitchers and catchers report this week."[1]

Kathie Hormby was a baseball fan who, in a cruel twist of irony, suffered from an ailment named after one of the game's greatest players: Lou Gehrig. Gehrig lived with amyotrophic lateral sclerosis (ALS), better known as Lou Gehrig's disease, for only two or three years. Kathie lived with the illness for eighteen years. Horick explains, "There was a symmetry about Kathie's illness, her faith and her love for baseball." As a devoted fan of the game, Kathie knew never to give up hope. Although her beloved Los Angeles Dodgers struggled for the last decade of Kathie's life, she knew that each spring brought a fresh start. Horick adds, "In baseball, as Kathie once wrote, as long as you can keep fouling off pitches, you're staying alive."[2]

Horick recalls that, on Kathie's final Sunday, she made one last contribution to the sharing of joys and concerns, telling the congregation, "Life begins on opening day." The pastor jokingly held up his Bible and replied, "Now Kathie, I missed where that's covered in here." Kathie's husband Dave then raised his voice and simply said, "Hope. That's in there."[3]

REVERSING THE CURSE

Hope, together with faith, is one of Paul's triad of virtues (not quite as good as love—1 Cor. 13:13). Elsewhere Paul explains that hope is born out of endurance: "We also boast in our sufferings, knowing that suffering produces endurance, and endurance produces character, and character produces hope, and hope does not disappoint us" (Rom. 5:3b–5a). In other words, Paul suggests that true hope is the result of one's hope being tested—that it is persistent. Such persistent hope is on display (and often pushed to the limit) in the stories of the Israelites wandering through Sinai en route to the promised land and of the people of Judah living in exile in Babylon. It is also on display in the stories of some of the most beloved franchises in Major League Baseball.

In 2004 the Boston Red Sox ended an eighty-six-year World Series drought after a dramatic seven-game victory over the New York Yankees in the American League Championship Series and a sweep of the St. Louis Cardinals in the Fall Classic. One year later, the Chicago White Sox brought an end to eighty-eight years of futility, sweeping the Houston Astros in the World Series. As of this writing, the Chicago Cubs have gone ninety-nine years without winning a title. Fans of the Cubbies or either color of Sox know anguish that has lasted even longer than the seventy or so years that the people of Judah spent in exile in Babylon. While being forced to live in a foreign land—after witnessing the destruction of the center of one's religious life—is far more severe than waiting for a baseball team to win a championship, the comparison isn't entirely ridiculous.

Red Sox fans took personally their team's inability to win in October and the supposed curse that kept them from realizing postseason success: the "curse of the Bambino." The Red Sox had won the World Series five times between 1903 and 1918. But after the 1919 season, the Sox sold star pitcher Babe Ruth—"the Bambino"—to the New York Yankees. Over the next eighty-four seasons, the Yankees won twenty-six World Series, the Sox won none, and Babe Ruth ended up being arguably the greatest major league player ever. Many Sox fans superstitiously or jokingly attributed their plight to a curse caused by the 1919 trade. For decades, New Englanders and other Sox faithful passed down Red Sox angst from generation to generation and told the stories of times when they came close but didn't get the job done: losses in the seventh games of the 1946, 1967, and 1975 World Series[4]; Bucky Dent's seventh-inning homer over the "Green Monster" at Fenway Park that gave the Yankees an edge over the Sox in a one-game playoff to determine which team would represent the American League East in the 1978 playoffs; Bill Buckner's fielding error in Game 6 of the 1986 World Series that enabled the New York Mets to tie the series and eventually win the title; Yankee Aaron Boone's game-winning, eleventh-inning home run in Game 7 of the 2003 American League Championship Series.[5]

Prior to the 2005 World Series, the Chicago White Sox hadn't won a title since 1917. The 1919 White Sox were the best team in the majors and were heavily favored to win the World Series over the Cincinnati Reds. But eight White Sox players agreed to throw the series to appease gambling interests. All eight players involved were banned from baseball for life. This scandal, known as the "Black Sox" scandal, was the subject of the popular movies *Eight Men Out* and *Field of Dreams*. Superstitious fans on the south side of Chicago came to believe in the "curse of the Black Sox"—the belief that, because the team willingly lost the 1919 series, they had not won the Series again for more than eight decades.

Fans on the north side of the Windy City have their own curse to contend with. The Cubs have suffered a longer championship drought than any other team in the history of major professional sports in the United States. The team has not won the World Series since 1908 and has not even played in the Series since 1945. (Fans of England's Preston North End football club arguably have suffered longer than even Cubs fans. Preston won the first two titles in the history of the English Football League First Division in 1889 and 1890 and has not won England's highest division since. On the other hand, Preston fans have been treated to three titles in the second highest division—most recently in 1951— and the 1938 FA Cup.) Some—again, superstitiously or jokingly—attribute this century of suffering to the "curse of the billy goat." According to the story, Billy Sianis, owner of a tavern near Wrigley Field (the Cubs' home stadium), had two tickets for Game 4 of the 1945 World Series (the last World Series featuring the Cubs). Sianis gave his extra ticket to his pet goat. Initially, Wrigley Field staff admitted the goat, but before the end of the game, stadium security ejected the cloven-hoofed mammal. Sianis took the ejection personally and apparently felt that the Cubs' rejection of his goat had something to do with the team losing Game 4, the series, and most of its games for the next two decades. While the Cubs' struggles began long before the goat incident, and though the team has managed to win a few division titles and make a handful of playoff appearances in recent decades, the team has nonetheless tried to symbolically reverse the curse. On opening day in both 1984 and 1989, the team invited Sianis' nephew to walk onto the field with a goat. Both of these seasons ended with the Cubs winning the National League East. The younger Sianis and the goat also made an appearance before a 1998 tiebreaker against the San Francisco Giants, which the Cubs won, earning a spot in the playoffs.

Despite the team's history of futility, the Cubs have had several promising teams in recent years. The 2003 Cubs were five outs away from the World Series before folding to the Florida Marlins in the eighth inning of Game 6 of the National League Championship Series. That was the game that made Steve Bartman a household name. Bartman was the fan sitting in the first row in the left field corner who caught a Luis Castillo foul ball in the eighth inning. Cubs left fielder Moises Alou may or may not have been able to make the catch and put the Cubs one out closer to victory if Bartman had not intervened. Instead, Castillo eventually drew a walk, and the Marlins scored eight runs to close out the inning. Many have blamed the Cubs' loss in the game and in the series at least in part on Bartman. At most, Bartman was partially responsible for one walk. No fan can be held responsible for giving up eight runs in a single inning. But Bartman, like the billy goat, became a symbol of the Cubs' travails.

Since 2003 the Cubs have twice won the National League Central Division, in 2007 and 2008. The 2008 team won ninety-seven games, more than any other team in the National League and the most for the Cubs since 1945. Both teams were swept in the first round of the playoffs, the National League Division Series. The Cubs have not won a postseason game since the Bartman incident.

Dennis Goodman, a roommate of mine in college and the most devoted Cubs fan I've known, says that the 2008 playoff loss was especially painful because the team was so good during the regular season. "An entirely different team showed up in the playoffs. All four infielders made an error in Game 2. I watch a lot of baseball and cannot remember the last time I have seen that." He remembers going to see the Cubs play the Braves in Game 3 of the 1998 National League Division Series, another postseason series in which the Cubs were swept. "When [the Braves' Greg] Maddox beat [the Cubs' Kerry] Wood to sweep out the Cubs, I remember walking by old men who were tearing up. It really stuck with me—like, holy cow, these guys have never seen a winner."

Those who have loved the Red Sox, White Sox, and Cubs and have made these teams a part of their lives have preserved these stories of curses and close calls and have embraced their underdog status. More importantly, these fans (most of them, anyway) have kept faith in their team. They've held on to hope. Dennis explains, "I literally watch parts of 145–150 [Cubs] games a year. At this point in my life, I would not know how to turn that off. And once the passion is there, of course you hope they win." He adds, "[Pascal] said that you should go ahead and believe in God because the penalty for not believing and being wrong is greater than [the penalty for] believing and it not being true. I guess to a certain extent that describes me with the Cubs. They will win it again at one point; I might as well be there when it happens." The ability of Sox and Cubs fans to keep the faith through decades of failures and close calls gives us a taste of what God's people endured during their years of wilderness wandering and exile.[6]

HOPE AMID EXILE

A good portion of what is now the Christian Old Testament was compiled during or after those decades in the sixth century B.C.E. when the leadership and upper classes of the people of Judah were living in exile in Babylon. The document that is now 1 and 2 Chronicles was likely written for Jews returning to Jerusalem from Babylonian captivity. Thus Chronicles devotes a lot of ink to genealogy, reminding the people that they trace their ancestry back to the patriarchs and matriarchs— Abraham and Sarah, Isaac and Rebekah, Jacob and Leah and Rachel— and that they are the heirs to God's promises to their forebears. God had promised to Abraham (who was called Abram at the time), "I will make of you a great nation, and I will bless you, and make your name great, so that you will be a blessing. I will bless those who bless you and the one who curses you I will curse; and in you all the families of the earth shall be blessed" (Gen. 12:2–3). God had reaffirmed this promise to Abraham's son Isaac, his grandson Jacob, his descendants who crossed the Jordan into the promised land, and eventually his descendants David and Solomon, under whom Israel realized its peak level of political and religious influence.

The returning exiles needed to remember their history and God's promises to them because they had become like the Chicago Cubs and their fans: a people far removed from their years of glory. Much as base-

ball fans wonder whether their favorite teams are cursed, the people of
Judah debated whether God's promises to them were still valid. God
had promised that a king from David's line would always sit on the
throne in Jerusalem (2 Sam. 7:1–17). How could God remain faithful
to this promise if Judah was under foreign rule? How could the people
hold onto hope when hope seemed lost? Much as Red Sox fans spent
their eighty-six-year "exile" telling their children stories about the
Bambino's curse, Bucky Dent, and Bill Buckner (along with tales of
Ted Williams, Carl Yastrzemski and Carlton Fisk's triumphs), God's
people told their children stories about Moses and Elijah and God's
covenant with David. One means of passing down these stories was
singing the hymns that have been compiled in the Book of Psalms.
Psalm 137 in particular captures the agony of a people anxiously await-
ing their return to glory:

> *How could we sing the LORD's song*
> *in a foreign land?*
> *If I forget you, O Jerusalem,*
> *let my right hand wither!*
> *Let my tongue cling to the roof of my mouth,*
> *if I do not remember you,*
> *if I do not set Jerusalem above my highest joy.* (verses 4–6)

Yet hope remained for Judah, just as it lingered in Red Sox nation.
One of Scripture's most powerful stories of hope involves the prophet
Jeremiah. As the Babylonian army laid siege to the city of Jerusalem
and carried the leaders of the people of Judah into exile, Jeremiah de-
cided to purchase property in the land that was currently being con-
quered (Jer. 32:1–15). His decision was suspect, ludicrous even, but
Jeremiah stood by it: "For thus says the LORD of hosts, the God of
Israel: Houses and fields and vineyards shall again be bought in this
land" (verse 15). Likewise, many Cubs fans have hope that World
Series tickets "shall again be bought in this land."

HOPE FOR A SEASON

One could argue that hope is elemental to religion, that religion itself
is the manifestation of hope—in the advent of a new age, in deliver-

ance, in redemption. One could also make the case that hope is elemental to being a true fan of any team. One cannot be a fan if he or she will not even consider the possibility that his or her team will exceed expectations or make a run at some significant accomplishment (such as making the playoffs, earning an invitation to a bowl game, or winning a division or conference). Even if a fan puts on a cynical, pessimistic front, telling friends that his or her beloved team is destined to spend an entire season at the bottom of the league, he or she must have some hope that this will not be the case.

The 2006 NFL season got off to an embarrassingly sad start for the Tennessee Titans and their fans. The Titans opened with a five-game losing streak that included a 40-7 loss to the San Diego Chargers and a 45–14 defeat at the hands of the Dallas Cowboys. (To the Titans' credit, in their fifth consecutive loss, they lost by only one point on the road against the Indianapolis Colts, the eventual Super Bowl champions.) On September 18, 2006, I wrote on my blog: "If you pay any attention to the NFL, I don't need to tell you how bad my Tennessee Titans are. Complaining at this point is too easy. Instead, fans need to focus on what the team can do right now to lessen the pain."[7] I then suggested that the team let go of coach Jeff Fisher,[8] trade respected veterans Keith Bulluck and Craig Hentrich (to spare them the suffering), give season-ticket holders tickets to a Baltimore Ravens game (so that they could watch all the former Titans who had signed with the Ravens prior to that season, specifically quarterback Steve McNair, wide receiver Derrick Mason, and cornerback Samari Rolle), and petition the NFL to create a developmental league for teams like the Titans. (I also advocated that the coaching staff go ahead and start rookie quarterback Vince Young. That turned out to be the right move.)

Despite my pain and my cynicism, I continued faithfully watching every Titans game. And even when the team was 0–5, I found myself thinking of scenarios by which the Titans could earn a playoff berth. I had hope that the Titans would turn their season around or at least give fans something to look forward to in 2007. I always had hope, no matter how hopeless the situation appeared to be.

That season, I did not hope in vain. The Titans won six of their final seven games to finish the season 8–8; rookie quarterback Vince

Young was named the league's Rookie of the Year. But even if the Titans hadn't redeemed what had seemed to be a lost season, another season would have come. The NFL Network used to run a commercial each year during the Super Bowl in which players whose teams didn't advance to the big game sing "Tomorrow" from the musical *Annie*. The commercial would conclude with the message, "Tomorrow, we're all undefeated again." Kathie Hormby knew and drew hope from this simple truth.

Of course, a person's spiritual journey cannot necessarily be neatly broken up into seasons, each offering the person a fresh start. Nor do most congregations or denominations have the luxury of knowing that, on a specific date, they will be able to put their pasts behind them and start anew. Nonetheless, new seasons and fresh starts are important truths in the Christian tradition. The best known scripture dealing with seasons is Ecclesiastes 3:1–8 (a popular passage made even more popular by the hit song "Turn! Turn! Turn!" written by Pete Seeger and famously recorded by the Byrds):

> *For everything there is a season, and a time for every matter*
>   *under heaven:*
> *a time to be born, and a time to die;*
> *a time to plant, and a time to pluck up what is planted;*
> *a time to kill, and a time to heal;*
> *a time to break down, and a time to build up;*
> *a time to weep, and a time to laugh;*
> *a time to mourn; and a time to dance;*
> *a time to throw away stones; and a time to gather stones together;*
> *a time to embrace, and a time to refrain from embracing;*
> *a time to seek, and a time to lose;*
> *a time to keep and a time to throw away;*
> *a time to tear, and a time to sew;*
> *a time to keep silence, and a time to speak;*
> *a time to love, and a time to hate;*
> *a time for war, and a time for peace.*

As sports fans know well, each season is different. No team wins a championship every year (though some teams—such as UCLA's men's basketball team in the 1960s and 1970s and the University of North Carolina's women's soccer team in the 1980s and 1990s—have had some extraordinarily long championship streaks). And very few teams are bad every year. Almost any season in any sport produces teams that exceed expectations and defy the experts' predictions. Consider the 2001–02 New Jersey Nets, who won their division and advanced to the NBA Finals despite finishing 26-56 the previous season and not having won a playoff series since 1984. Or the 1995 Northwestern University football team. Prior to that season, Northwestern had only played in one bowl game in the school's history—the 1949 Rose Bowl. (Northwestern actually won the 1948 Rose Bowl, beating California (Berkeley) 20–14. For many years the Wildcats, perennial bottom feeders in the Big Ten Conference, could boast the league's best postseason winning percentage: 1–0.) In 1995 the Wildcats, who had finished near the bottom of the Big Ten Conference for much of the previous three decades, won the conference, beating perennial powers Michigan and Penn State along the way. Northwestern ended the regular season ranked in the top ten and earned a spot in the Rose Bowl.[9] In sports, almost every season comes with surprises, and no fan can safely assume that his or her team's next season will end a certain way.

But more important than the seasons themselves is the opportunity to start anew. At the beginning of each season in team sports, every team is 0–0: winless and undefeated with a winning percentage that mathematically does not exist. Each team has an opportunity to end the season by winning a championship. Christians believe that, through Christ, we also get an opportunity to start again. Paul writes in 2 Corinthians 5:17, "So if anyone is in Christ, there is a new creation: everything old has passed away; see, everything has become new!" In John's Gospel Jesus tells the Pharisee Nicodemus, "Very truly, I tell you, no one can see the kingdom of God without being born from above" (John 3:3); Nicodemus, taking Jesus's teaching literally, is confused by the concept of being "born again," prompting Jesus to explain salvation in more direct terms. The prophet Ezekiel twice tells of God's plans to redeem God's people by replacing their "heart of stone" with a "heart of flesh" (Ezek. 11:19; 36:26).

Being re-created or reborn is a key aspect of any Christian's faith journey, whether this rebirth occurs (as some suggest) in a single transcendent life-altering experience or (as others insist) continually through the persistent prodding of God's grace. Christians celebrate rebirth and renewal especially in the sacrament of baptism. While interpretations of baptism vary across the many different Christian traditions and communities, many Christians in antiquity considered baptism a ritual of death (sinking beneath the baptismal waters representing the entombment of one's former life of sin) and resurrection (emerging from the waters representing taking on a new life, free from sin). The newly baptized converts thus began a new season, 0–0.[10] Modern interpretations of baptism retain this emphasis on new birth. The Articles of Religion of the Methodist Church[11] say that "Baptism is not only a sign of profession and mark of difference whereby Christians are distinguished from others . . . ; but it is also a sign of regeneration or the new birth."[12]

The defining event in the Christian story is, of course, Christ's resurrection. In the Gospels Jesus foreshadows his resurrection by bringing back to life Jairus' daughter (Mark 5:21–43) and Lazarus (John 11:1–44). These miracle stories, along with other biblical resurrections such as Elijah reviving the widow of Zarephath's son (1 Kings 17:17–24), are extraordinary stories of hope in their own right. But Christians profess that Christ's resurrection is uniquely significant. Unlike Lazarus and Jairus's daughter, who would die again, Jesus defeated death by returning from the grave with a body that was eternal and uncorruptible. His resurrection signified the ultimate hope for every flawed and sinful human being. Paul writes to the Christian community in Rome, "For the law of the Spirit of life in Christ Jesus has set you free from the law of sin and of death" (Rom. 8:2). Thus no one need be held captive by sin. Even if one is mathematically eliminated from the playoffs before the all-star break (in the figurative sense), by God's grace and through Christ's death and resurrection, one can leave these failings behind and look forward to a new season.

A PEOPLE OF HOPE

Kathie Hormby knew the importance of hope, both as a Christian and as a sports fan. Fans of the Chicago Cubs continue to illustrate how hope can carry a people through decades (even a century) of adversity. And my hope that the Tennessee Titans will once again be a contender in the NFL is renewed at the beginning of each football season.

People who follow and care about sports know all about hope. They know that, at the beginning of every season, their team has a chance to end that season with a championship; and they know that, no matter how poorly their team performs, they can look forward to another season. Sports fans persist in their hope by telling stories of past triumphs and disappointments, knowing that one day their team will relive its past glory or finally exorcise its demons.

Christians, like sports fans, are a people of hope. The story of God's people is one of hope that persists through frustration and uncertainty. For Christians, this story reaches its climax with the resurrection of Jesus Christ, an event that gave hopelessly sinful human beings hope for new life and new beginnings.

2

DAVIDS AND GOLIATHS

Why Everyone Loves an Underdog

*You're five foot nothin'. A hundred and nothin'.
And you have barely a speck of athletic ability. And you hung in
there with the best college football players in the land for two
years. You're gonna walk outta here with a degree from the
University of Notre Dame. In this life, you don't have
to prove nothin' to nobody but yourself.*

—**CHARLES S. DUTTON** as Fortune in *Rudy*

*David put his hand in his bag, took out a stone, slung it,
and struck the Philistine on his forehead; the stone sank into
his forehead, and he fell face down on the ground.*

—**1 SAMUEL 17:49**

THE MOST UBIQUITOUS BIBLICAL NARRATIVE IN SPORTS

The most ubiquitous biblical narrative among sports broadcasters and writers is the well-worn tale of David and Goliath (1 Sam. 17): David, though he has been anointed the next king of Israel, is just a boy. Yet he volunteers to take on Goliath the giant—the champion sent out by the

Philistines, the Mediterranean coastal nation that gave Israel so many fits during the late Bronze Age. Goliath, depending on which ancient manuscript you trust, is either six-foot-nine or nine-foot-six (two feet taller than NBA player Yao Ming); his head, torso, and legs are covered in fine bronze armor; he wields a spear whose iron head weighs "six hundred shekels"; and he even has a personal shield bearer. King Saul attempts to arm David in a similar fashion, but the young warrior is unable to walk when laden with bronze battle gear. Thus, David approaches the Philistine giant armed only with a staff, a sling, and five smooth stones.

Goliath meets his challenger with trash talk that would make Gary Payton proud. David responds by affirming his allegiance to the God of Israel and boldly declares:

> "This very day the LORD will deliver you into my hand, and I will strike you down and cut off your head; and I will give the dead bodies of the Philistine army this very day to the birds of the air and to the wild animals of the earth, so that all the earth may know that there is a God in Israel, and that all this assembly may know that the LORD does not save by sword and spear; for the battle is the LORD's and he will give you into our hand." (1 Sam. 17:46–47)

Again, Gary Payton would be impressed.

Of course, as so many Sunday school graduates know, David is true to his seemingly arrogant and preposterous words. He takes down the giant with his sling and one stone and then decapitates Goliath with Goliath's own sword.[1]

Stephen Prothero, who includes a Dictionary of Religious Literacy in his book *Religious Literacy: What Every American Needs to Know—and Doesn't,* writes in his entry for David and Goliath, "This story provides the template for hundreds of Hollywood sports movies—a template made explicit in the film *Hoosiers* (1986)."[2] ("Hundreds" is a bit of an overstatement, but you get the point.) In *Hoosiers*, set in the early 1950s, tiny Hickory High School in southern Indiana wins the coveted state basketball championship, defeating a bigger, more athletic, and more celebrated team from South Bend in the title game. The story is based loosely on Milan High School's real-life title run in 1955. Milan defeated perennial Indiana basketball powerhouse Muncie Central in the final.

In the film, as the Hickory Huskers are gathered in the locker room prior to the championship game, the town's minister leads them in a pregame devotion. (Apparently, in the fictional town of Hickory, Indiana, there is only one church, and thus one minister, of note. The minister's son, Strap, happens to be on the team.) The minister chooses to read aloud from the story of David and Goliath. Presumably, Hickory—with its small student body and lackluster facilities—plays the role of David. South Bend Central by contrast—the big city school with a rich tradition of success in the state tournament—is Goliath.

The metaphor breaks down there. We have no indication that the South Bend Central Bears (or the Muncie Central players on whom they are based) taunted their less esteemed competitors. And the Indiana High School Athletic Association's state basketball championship is not exactly a battle between the godly and godless. Significantly, in contrast to the all-white Hickory Huskers, the South Bend team in the movie fields a predominantly African American roster. Using the David-Goliath story to describe this match-up is racially problematic, setting up a contest between the good, humble, white country team and the big, bad, African American city team.

NOBODY WANTS TO BE A GOLIATH

The David-Goliath metaphor, when applied to sports, often does a disservice to the team or player who plays the Goliath role. Scripture tells us that Goliath is a bad dude who owes his advantage over David largely to his considerable size and superior weapons and armor. Goliath is a grown man, while David is but a boy—a boy without the strength even to wear armor. David owes his unlikely victory as much to his opponent's arrogance as to his own skill. People of faith, of course, assert that David owes his victory to God, rather than his abilities or his adversary's haughtiness. Thus God is on the side of the boy. In sports, by contrast, rarely does one side have the upper hand in terms of moral superiority or divine favor.

Consider George Mason University's unlikely win over Connecticut to advance to the Final Four in the 2006 NCAA (National Collegiate

Athletic Association) men's basketball tournament. Some sports aficionados rank the game—or George Mason's tournament run in general—among the great upsets in history. Only one team seeded as low as that 2006 George Mason team had advanced to the Final Four. To what extent is the Patriots' victory over mighty UConn a David-and-Goliath story?

When the two teams met in the regional finals (Elite Eight) of the NCAA tournament, Connecticut was the obvious favorite, as the Huskies had been ranked at or near the top of the college basketball polls for the entire season, had won two titles in the previous seven seasons, and hailed from one of the nation's strongest basketball conferences, the Big East. On the whole, Connecticut's big men were bigger than George Mason's, and their guards were more athletic. On the other hand, George Mason did have solid big men and athletic guards (even if they weren't projected first-round NBA draft picks), not to mention quality bench players and outstanding senior leadership. While Mason came out of the lowly Colonial Athletic Association (and barely got a tournament bid), they had proven themselves against quality competition during the 2005–06 season, defeating a highly regarded Wichita State team and narrowly losing to major-conference powers Mississippi State and Wake Forest. That season, George Mason briefly earned a spot in the ESPN/USA Today Top 25 Coaches Poll.

So the disparity between George Mason and Connecticut wasn't nearly as stark as that between David and the Philistine champion. More importantly, Connecticut's performance in the 2006 NCAA tourney was much more inspired that Goliath's performance on that battlefield in Palestine. Sure, many experts had picked the Huskies to win the title; but rarely if ever is there an obvious favorite to win the Big Dance, and no team should ever be disappointed about having advanced to the Elite Eight. And UConn almost pulled out the victory after an impressive second-half surge that pushed the game into overtime. (The fact that George Mason managed to win in overtime after Connecticut came back to tie the game at the end of regulation made the Patriots' victory that much more impressive.) Goliath's defeat was an embarrassment; Connecticut's defeat was the conclusion of a pretty good season.

Like the Philistine giant, many favorites in sports owe their status in part to good genes (insofar as genetics determines size, build, reflexes, and so forth) and superior resources. (Consider, for example, the palatial new practice facilities that the University of Kentucky built for its basketball program.[3]) Yet, most teams and athletes considered favorites among their peers also owe their status to hard work, good coaching, and experience. It's easy to discount the achievements of perennial powerhouses in college basketball (for instance, Duke and North Carolina's men's teams and Tennessee and Connecticut's women's teams) and football (USC and Florida) because these teams seem to have easy access to the nation's best players and coaches. Too often we forget that these players have become some of the nation's best through years of practice and dedication. We forget the work and commitment that is necessary for these players to have an opportunity to play for a team that will be favored to advance to the Final Four or play in a BCS bowl game. In professional team sports the franchises that become perennial contenders are often those that are able to develop their weaker, less celebrated players (such as the NBA's San Antonio Spurs or the NFL's New England Patriots in the first decade of the twenty-first century). Referring to athletic powers as "Goliath" cheapens all that these athletes have done to become teams (or players, runners, and so forth) that are expected to win.

For that matter, "David" may not be an apt description of many of the great underdogs in sports history. The athlete most analogous to David may have been tennis player Michael Chang. Chang was one of several great American tennis players to come of age in the late 1980s and early 1990s. Although he would be overshadowed by more successful peers Pete Sampras, Andre Agassi, and Jim Courier, Chang was the first of his "class" to win a Grand Slam tournament when he made an inspired run to the title in the 1989 French Open. Chang was not entirely unknown at the time: He was seeded fifteenth in the 1989 French. But Chang was only seventeen years old and could have passed for fourteen. His opponent, Sweden's Stefan Edberg, was seeded third, had three Grand Slam titles to his credit, and was barely more than year away from becoming the world's top-ranked player. Edberg's size and build made very obvious that he was far more physically mature than the boyish Chang. Chang, like David, emerged from this boy-versus-man bout victorious.

Although Chang is still the youngest player to win a men's Grand Slam singles title, his match against Stefan Edberg was hardly a mismatch of Davidic proportions. For one, most sports (by their very nature) mandate a certain level of equality. In tennis, for example, both players are allowed a racket and have the same amount of space on the court to cover. Tennis is also a young man's game. Tennis players are considered "old" when they reach their late twenties, an age at which many professional athletes are hitting their prime. Tennis is also a game in which speed and agility are more valuable than the brawn that comes with physical maturity. The Davids of sports rarely are at disadvantage comparable to that of the biblical David.

Consider also that David defeats the Philistine in a short, lopsided battle. David executes two plays—one using a sling and one using a sword. Goliath doesn't even get off a play. The fight itself is anticlimactic, lacking in drama and competition. The great underdog stories in sports tend to culminate in an intense competition—often one that is in doubt until the very end. Boise State's groundbreaking victory over perennial power Oklahoma in the 2007 Fiesta Bowl required last-second trickery and overtime heroics on the part of the underdog Broncos. Villanova's upset of Georgetown in the 1985 NCAA tourney was in doubt until the game's final seconds. Zach Johnson's unlikely win at the 2007 Masters was the result of four days of struggle in cool, windy spring weather that made the course unusually difficult, and of outlasting world number one Tiger Woods, who had taken the lead early on the last day. The Boston Red Sox, whose postseason struggles are legendary, fell behind 3–0 and needed seven games to defeat the New York Yankees, whose postseason triumphs are legendary, in the 2004 American League Championship Series.

Regarding the giant's legendary arrogance, there is no consistent pattern of the "Goliaths" in the sporting world taunting the lowly "Davids" who ultimately bring them down. Bobby Riggs might be the rare example of a truly arrogant Goliath. In 1973 the former tennis star—Riggs won Wimbledon in 1939 and was one of the world's best players in the 1940s—challenged women's tennis champ Billie Jean King to the much publicized Battle of the Sexes. Riggs was renowned for his bravado, but his haughtiness may have had more to do with showmanship than with genuine arrogance. At any rate, comparing the Battle of the Sexes to David's battle with Goliath may be unwarranted because Riggs was not necessarily the clear favorite. Though Riggs had easily defeated Margaret Court (at the time, the world's top-ranked female player) earlier that year, Riggs was fifty-five years old and retired from professional tennis; King, on the other hand, was in her prime. If nothing else, the comparison is partially valid because King defeated Riggs nearly as soundly as David felled Goliath, winning the match in straight sets, 6–4, 6–3, 6–3.[4]

In the case of Super Bowl III, at the time known as the 1968 AFL-NFL Championship Game, the team in the David role is the one remembered for its arrogance. Actually, the underdog New York Jets, as a team, were not necessarily cocky, but their quarterback Joe Namath certainly was. Namath was known for his swagger and was not interested in critics who claimed that the talent in the AFL (the Jets' league at the time) was not on par with that in the NFL, the league of the favored Baltimore Colts. The Colts were eighteen-point favorites. Three days before the game, Namath famously said in public, "We're going to win the game. I guarantee it." Analysts and fans ridiculed Namath's guarantee, but the Jets nonetheless upset the Colts 16–7.

Perhaps the story that best fits the David-Goliath mold is the United States Hockey Team's victory over the Soviet Union in the semifinals of the medal round in the 1980 Olympics. Against the backdrop of the Cold War, the game took on good-versus-evil overtones. It was a form of representative combat: the Cold War on ice. Classifying the Soviet players as evil—even if one feels that way about the former Soviet government—is unfair. We need to remember that the players in this game of seemingly international significance were kids. Still, the players in this storied contest were representing competing ideologies that featured, in part, a vast difference in approach to defining the word" amateur" in sports. And much as David's victory over Goliath gave hope to a nation in crisis, the U.S. Hockey Team's unlikely victory over the Soviets lifted the spirits of an entire country. And the presumed disparity in talent was arguably as close as major, modern sports have come to a mismatch on the level of David and Goliath.

"LET US RUN WITH PERSEVERANCE"

Maybe I'm asking too much of the metaphor, but I think that the sporting world alludes to the David-Goliath story far more often than it should. Such comparisons usually sell short the often worthy accomplishments of the player or team in the Goliath role and understate the drama of the contest itself. Most successful underdogs achieve their success through (among other things) faith and perseverance, two virtues lauded both by the Apostle Paul and the author of Hebrews. (See, for instance, Romans 4:13–25 and Hebrews 12:1–3.) Perseverance is persistently and tenaciously pursuing a certain goal or objective; it is a mix of devotion and endurance, a willingness to continue despite all adversity toward a goal. Hebrews 12:1–3 famously uses sports imagery to communicate the value of perseverance:

> Therefore, since we are surrounded by so great a cloud of witnesses, let us also lay aside every weight and the sin that clings so closely, and let us run with perseverance the race that is set before us, looking to Jesus the pioneer and perfecter of our faith, who for the sake of the joy that was set before him endured the cross, disregarding its shame, and has taken his seat at the right hand of the throne of God. Consider him who endured such hostility against himself from sinners, so that you may not grow weary or lose heart.

With all due respect to the young shepherd boy who took down the armored giant, the story of David's battle with Goliath does not show us the sort of perseverance that makes so many underdogs incredible. The movie *Hoosiers*, which so famously and prominently features the David-Goliath story, is a great movie because it is so much more than just a David-Goliath moment. We love the Hickory Huskers not only because Jimmy Chitwood hit the final shot to clinch a victory in the state championship game over the heavily favored South Bend team, but also because of the journey the team traveled to get its title shot. For the fictional Hickory Huskers, this journey involved beginning the season with only six players, having the townspeople demand that Coach Norman Dale (played by Gene Hackman) be fired, and dealing with the inconsistent behavior of Shooter (the town-drunk-turned-assistant-coach played by Dennis Hopper). The real-life George Mason University Patriots first had to bite their nails while the NCAA Tournament selection committee decided if the team would even get a bid to the Big Dance. Then they had to beat perennial power Michigan State without star guard Tony Skinn (who had been suspended for hitting a Hofstra player in the groin). After that, they upset a heavily favored North Carolina team before getting their signature win over Connecticut.

Maybe the most memorable illustration of perseverance in the world of sports comes from another film written and directed by the team responsible for Hoosiers. *Rudy* (1993) is based on the true story of Daniel "Rudy" Ruettiger. In the early 1970s Reuttiger decided to pursue his lifelong dream of playing football for the University of Notre Dame, home to a storied football program that recently had won two consensus national championships under then coach Ara Parseghian. Reuttiger had been an effective defensive player for Joliet Catholic High School outside Chicago, but Rudy's small stature—he stood five foot six and weighed only 165 pounds[5]—made him invisible to major college recruiters. Still, Rudy was determined to play for the Fighting Irish.

Size and strength weren't the only factors keeping Rudy from playing for Notre Dame. Notre Dame had (and continues to have) high academic standards, even for scholarship athletes. As an aspiring walk-on, Rudy had to rely on his academic record alone to earn admission. Rudy's high school grades and brief time in the Navy were not sufficient for Notre Dame, so he began his quest to play for the Irish at Holy Cross Junior College, located near the Notre Dame campus in South Bend, Indiana. While he was a student at Holy Cross, Rudy learned that he was dyslexic. His application to Notre Dame was rejected three times before he finally gained admission.

Enrolling at Notre Dame was only the first phase of Rudy's quest to put on the Golden Dome and run onto the field of Notre Dame Stadium under the watch of Touchdown Jesus. Reuttiger was still too small to have a realistic chance of making even the Fighting Irish practice squad. But he tried out anyway and earned the favor of assistant coach Merv Johnson, who allowed Rudy to be a part of Notre Dame's scout team. After two full seasons on the scout team, Rudy finally got the chance to dress for a game—the final game of his senior season, against Georgia Tech on November 8, 1975. While the movie exaggerates certain details surrounding the game—every member of the varsity team did not lay down his jersey and ask that Rudy play in his place, and the crowd didn't chant Rudy's name until he got a chance to play—Rudy did record a sack on the game's final play, and his teammates did carry him off the field. No other college football player has become such a legend for recording one sack in his entire career, and that on the final play of a game that had already been decided.

Rudy's is the consummate underdog story: A kid with limited abilities and resources becomes an American sports icon. We remember Rudy and tell his story because of what he went through and overcame. Daniel Ruettiger persevered, taking on several physical and academic challenges along the way. One character in the movie, Fortune, a groundskeeper (who is actually based on a handful of different people who influenced Reuttiger during his time at Notre Dame), memorably articulates the distinction of Rudy's accomplishment when Reuttiger is considering giving up on his goal to dress for the varsity team: "You're five foot nothin'. A hundred and nothin'. And you have barely a speck of athletic ability. And you hung in there with the best college football players in the land for two years. You're gonna walk outta here with a degree from the University of Notre Dame. In this life, you don't have to prove nothin' to nobody but yourself."[6]

Rudy is known more for his journey than the destination to which it led. This sets him apart from other beloved underdogs. We remember Milan High School's state championship win over powerhouse Muncie Central and the U.S. Hockey Team's upset of the Soviet Union in the semifinals of the medal round. While the movies *Hoosiers* and *Miracle*, respectively, remind us of the roads these teams traveled to achieve glory, we tend to identify these teams with a moment—with a single game or tournament. Rudy's much celebrated journey reminds us that these incredible moments don't just happen; they are the result of considerable effort and struggle. Underdogs don't just appear; they persevere.

Perseverance plays a role in many of the Bible's grand narratives: Abram and Sarai (later Abraham and Sarah) faithfully followed God's instructions for decades before God's promise to give the couple a son was finally fulfilled. Joseph came into Israel as a slave, was wrongly accused of seducing a high-ranking official's wife and thrown in prison, but ultimately became the Pharaoh's right-hand man and was able to save the nation from years of drought. The people of Judah spent nearly seventy years in exile in Babylon; and when they were finally liberated by the Persians, they still had to rebuild the temple. But these people managed to build a temple that was even more glorious than the one the Babylonians had destroyed. Paul's mission to the Gentiles was fraught with imprisonment, persecution, and even a shipwreck, but Paul was nonetheless able to establish healthy churches throughout the Roman world. Seldom in Scripture are God's promises fulfilled immediately or without the recipients of these promises enduring trials and challenges.

A PERSISTENT FAITH

While the story of David's battle against Goliath teaches a valuable lesson about having faith in the moment, many of our beloved athletic underdogs teach us about a more persistent faith, a faith that endures over time and through highs and lows. Such faith is on display in the story of the Hebrews' exodus from Egypt and subsequent wandering in the wilderness. Trusting Moses and Aaron as they made their initial stand against the Pharaoh and following the brothers' instructions for the first Passover certainly required faith. Sticking with Moses and Aaron through forty years in the Sinai wilderness required even greater faith—faith that was tested on many occasions during the Israelites' sojourn. This saga features such memorable episodes as the manna from heaven,[7] the golden calf,[8] the spies sent to Canaan,[9] and the water from the rock.[10] In fact, the wandering Israelites may be better known for their lapses in faith than for their fidelity to God. But even after being punished and nearly rejected by God, the people follow Moses (if sometimes reluctantly) and continue their journey.

Israel's escape from Egypt and journey to the promised land may be a more apt parallel to the current-day triumphs of sporting underdogs.

But instead of comparing the story of God's people to Milan High School's 1954 state championship run or the United States Hockey Team's Olympic triumph in 1980, we should look to all of these stories as illustrations of faith in their own right.

The U.S. Hockey Team's unlikely victory over the Soviet Union was a religious experience of sorts for broadcaster Al Michaels, who famously exclaimed, "Do you believe in miracles? Yes!" Prior to the Olympics, the Soviets had routed an NHL all-star team 6–0 and had beaten the American team 10–3 in an exhibition game. During the opening round of Olympic play, the U.S.S.R. team went undefeated, 5–0, beating Japan 16–0 and the Netherlands 17–4.

Without interviewing the assortment of college hockey players and other amateurs on the U.S. team's roster, one cannot know the role of faith (whether of the religious variety or in the more general sense of the word) in the team's performance. But the faith of the athletes themselves is incidental to what they can teach fans and observers about faith. After Jesus dampens a wealthy young man's spirits by telling him that he can only "have eternal life" by selling his possessions and giving the money to the poor (Matt. 19:16–22), his disciples ask, "Then who can be saved?" (19:25). Jesus replies, "For God all things are possible" (19:26). The U.S. Hockey Team gave us a memorable illustration of this simple but incredible truth.

Without suggesting that God has willed certain underdogs to victory, we can look to these unlikely champions as reminders that "all things are possible." Certainly, David's victory over the Philistine also gives us such assurance. But underdogs in sports show us that the impossible doesn't necessarily become possible in an instant. Generally, the underdogs who are successful are working hard toward their goal long before the season starts; to reach their goal, they must sustain this level of devotion throughout a season or career. Victorious underdogs must also have faith that they can and will achieve what they have set out to do.

Too often, I think, Christians wrongly equate faith and belief. Christians over the centuries have mistakenly derived this equivalence from Paul's epistles. Paul pairs faith with grace and contrasts faith with works, giving many readers the impression that "faith" is the part of religion that doesn't involve doing anything. But Scripture is clear that faith is an active virtue. The Letter of James says:

> What good is it, my brothers and sisters, if you say you have faith but do not have works? Can faith save you? If a brother or sister is naked and lacks daily food, and one of you says to them, 'Go in peace; keep warm and eat your fill,' and yet you do not supply their bodily needs, what is the good of that? So faith by itself, if it has no works, is dead." (James 2:14–17)

(To be fair, to suggest that Paul considers "faith" and "works" distinct or even mutually exclusive is a misreading of Paul. Paul is very concerned about the actions and behaviors of people in the churches with whom he communicates. Specifically, he teaches that certain behaviors are the inevitable result of believing in Christ and accepting God's grace. See, for example, Paul's description of a true Christian in Romans 12:9–21 and his list of the "fruit of the Spirit" in Galatians 5:22–23.)

The New Testament teaches us that faith should be active. And we see active faith at play in the stories of unlikely champions. If an athlete or a team is to win or to succeed on some level, she or he or they must believe in her or his or their ability to realize such success. But this belief is moot unless it is lived. Underdogs who win championships or break down barriers must believe that they can exceed expectations and act on that belief. Their achievements then give fans and spectators faith that, indeed, "all things are possible."

USE DAVID AND GOLIATH WITH CAUTION

I would advise that sports commentators and broadcasters exercise caution when comparing what they witness on the field to the battle between David and Goliath. Such a comparison may cast a negative light on the often commendable accomplishments of the fallen favorites and overemphasize a team or athlete's moment of victory at the expense of that team or athlete's often inspiring journey.

Instead of using a familiar Bible story to interpret the triumphs of sporting underdogs, we should look to the stories of these underdogs as illustrations of perseverance and faith. Surprise champions (such as the 1980 U.S. Hockey Team), contenders (such as the 2006 George Mason Patriots), and overachievers (such as Daniel "Rudy" Ruettiger) inspire us to persevere when we face adversity and low expectations, to have faith that we can accomplish extraordinary things, and to act on that faith.

3

NEITHER JEW NOR GREEK, SLAVE NOR FREE

We're All One on Game Day

Champion of the world. A Black boy. Some Black mother's son.
He was the strongest man in the world. People drank Coca-Colas
like ambrosia and ate candy bars like Christmas.

—MAYA ANGELOU, *KNOW WHY THE CAGED BIRD SINGS*,
on Joe Louis winning the heavyweight title in 1935

There is no longer Jew or Greek, there is no longer
slave or free, there is no longer male and female;
for all of you are one in Christ Jesus.

—GALATIANS 3:28

BREAKING THE COLOR BARRIER

In 1997 Major League Baseball officially retired the number 42 in honor of Jackie Robinson, who had broken baseball's "color barrier" fifty years earlier. It is customary for individual teams to retire a number. (Duke University's men's basketball team, for instance, is getting dangerously close to not having enough eligible numbers to cover its roster.[1]) An entire professional league retiring a number is unprecedented. Jackie Robinson was unprecedented.

On April 15, 1947, Robinson debuted at second base for the Brooklyn Dodgers, making him the first African American player to play in the major leagues. Since the 1880s, Major League Baseball and its minor-league affiliates had upheld an unwritten policy of discrimination. Kenesaw Mountain Landis, baseball commissioner from 1920 until his death in 1944, blocked several attempts to integrate the game. Reasons given to justify segregation varied. There was fear that some star players would quit if they were forced to play and travel with black players. While some cities would be amenable to having African American players on their teams, others would not, including southern and Midwestern cities with minor-league franchises. As the possibility of integrating baseball grew, some owners and executives suddenly became concerned about the fate of the Negro leagues. What would happen to the Kansas City Monarchs and the Homestead Grays if Major League Baseball signed all of their best players to big contracts? Interestingly, most everyone who was worried about the fate of the Negro leagues was white. African American ballplayers and officials welcomed integration.

In 1945, less than a year after Landis's death, Brooklyn Dodgers General Manager Branch Rickey signed Robinson and sent him to play with the Dodgers' minor-league affiliate in Montreal. Rickey had undertaken an exhaustive search to find the perfect player to break the color barrier. He wanted a player with undeniable talent and undeniable character—someone with enough strength and dignity to take the field each day amid boos from fans and taunts from opposing players.[2] When Rickey signed Robinson, critics said that the Dodgers executive was motivated only by profit and winning ball games, that racial justice was just a side effect.[3]

Robinson, in his autobiography *I Never Had It Made*, defends Rickey. He introduces his former general manager by telling a story about Rickey's days as a baseball coach at Ohio Wesleyan University. In 1910 Rickey's team was on the road in South Bend, Indiana, and the manager of the hotel where the team was staying refused to give a room to Charley Thomas, the team's only African American player. Rickey suggested a compromise, and hotel management reluctantly allowed Thomas to sleep on a cot in Rickey's room.

Robinson recalls Rickey's response to this injustice:

"[Thomas] sat on that cot," Mr. Rickey said, "and was silent for a long time. Then he began to cry, tears he couldn't hold back. . . . I sat and watched him, not knowing what to do until he began tearing at one hand with the other—just as if he were trying to scratch the skin off his hands with his fingernails. . . . 'It's my hands,' he sobbed, 'They're black. If only they were white, I'd be as good as anybody then, wouldn't I, Mr. Rickey? If only they were white.'"

"Charley," Mr. Rickey said, "the day will come when they won't have to be white."[4]

And that day came, though it came long after Jackie Robinson's debut with the Dodgers.

Robinson's first seasons with the Dodgers were unpleasant. He heard taunts and racial epithets from fans and opposing players alike, few of which had anything to do with his performance on the field, which was exemplary from the start. But the trials of Robinson's early career actually served to unite him and the rest of his Brooklyn Dodgers teammates. In his autobiography Robinson mentions specifically Philadelphia Phillies manager Ben Chapman, who notoriously tried to provoke Robinson (and several other players, based on these players' nationalities). Chapman's verbal assaults were so hateful and hurtful that, according to Rickey, "Chapman did more than anybody to unite the Dodgers. When he poured out that string of unconscionable abuse, he solidified and unified thirty men, not one of whom was willing to sit by and see someone kick around a man who had his hands tied behind his back."[5]

While outside prejudices rallied Robinson's Dodgers teammates around their groundbreaking infielder, Robinson's play on the field endeared him to baseball writers, who voted him Major League Baseball's Rookie of the Year in 1947 and the National League's Most Valuable Player (MVP) in 1949. In 1962 they elected Robinson to the Baseball Hall of Fame on the first ballot. And all sorts of people enjoyed listening to the hit song "Did You See Jackie Robinson Hit That Ball?" written by Buddy Johnson and performed by Count Basie. (The song is available through iTunes and other online music stores.) A movie, *The Jackie Robinson Story*, starring Robinson as himself, hit theaters in 1950. Throughout his career and into the years following his retirement, Robinson grew in popularity, particularly among white Americans. He also became a respected voice in American politics, holding both parties accountable to their approach to civil rights and race relations.

When God sent Samuel to anoint one of Jesse's sons the next king of Israel, Jesse did not consider the possibility that his youngest son, David, would be chosen over his older and more physically impressive brothers. But God said to Samuel, "Do not look on his appearance or on the height of his stature, because I have rejected him; for the LORD does not see as mortals see; they look on the outward appearance, but the LORD looks on the heart" (1 Sam. 16:7). While neither race nor ethnicity is the subject of this particular verse, the truth that God is concerned with the heart, and not one's outer appearance, speaks to prejudice and discrimination based on skin color. Branch Rickey saw beyond the outer appearance of Robinson and other ballplayers and focused on the talent and ambition that could help his team win the pennant.

. . . AND THE CULTURE BARRIER

African Americans weren't the only ones to face and overcome prejudice in baseball. In the 1950s baseball saw an influx of players from Puerto Rico, Cuba, Dominican Republic, and Venezuela. Puerto Rico's Roberto Clemente made his major league debut with the Pittsburgh Pirates eight years after Jackie Robinson broke the color barrier and went on to become the game's first Latino superstar. As a black player from Puerto Rico, Clemente had trouble finding his place in American society. Because of the color of his skin, Clemente was subject to all the Jim Crow laws and racist attitudes that made African Americans second-class citizens. This sort of prejudice was difficult for him to grasp. But differences in language and culture kept the star outfielder, along with other Latino players, from fitting in with African Americans. According to sportswriter Juan Gonzalez, "There was an attempt to really sort of deny the Latino heritage of these ballplayers." He recalls

Roberto being called "Bobby" by a press corps that wanted to Americanize him.[6] As the numbers of Latino players in the majors grew throughout the sixties and seventies, there was a backlash. In the mid sixties, San Francisco Giants manager Herman Franks banned the speaking of Spanish in the clubhouse.[7]

Clemente was discouraged by the prejudice he faced early in his career. He didn't understand why he finished eighth in National League MVP voting in 1960 when he felt that he should have been a favorite to win the award. (That year Clemente's Pirates shocked the baseball world by upsetting the star-laden New York Yankees in the World Series; many analysts compared the outcome of the series to David's defeat of Goliath.[8]) But as his career progressed, Clemente's play on the field won over fans in Pittsburgh and elsewhere. Not only was he an icon in his native Puerto Rico; Clemente also forced mainland Americans to rethink their prejudices toward Latinos. He was heavily involved in the civil rights movement of the 1960s and spent considerable time in the off-season assisting impoverished people in Latin America. In 1966 he did win the National League MVP, and when the Pirates returned to the World Series in 1971 they had a diverse team of white, black, and Latino players. After the Pirates won the series and the press flocked to interview Clemente, the recently crowed World Series MVP insisted on speaking to his family and fellow Latinos in Spanish. For an athlete in a major American sport to speak unapologetically to the press in a language other than English was unprecedented. When Clemente came into the majors, fans had trouble accepting a dark-skinned, Spanish-speaking outfielder and didn't care for players who were looking to make a social statement. By the end of his career, Clemente the bilingual activist was one of the game's most beloved players.

Sadly, Roberto Clemente died on New Year's Eve 1972 at the age of thirty-eight. He was on his way to Nicaragua to deliver relief supplies to earthquake victims when his plane went down. His body was never recovered. Clemente was elected to the Baseball Hall of Fame in 1973, the first Latino player to earn that honor and only the second player for whom the mandatory five-year waiting period was waived (the first was Lou Gehrig). Like Robinson before him, Clemente proved that a player could be one of the game's best and appeal to fans regardless of race, ethnicity, or cultural heritage.

A NEARLY IDEAL VENUE FOR ADDRESSING PREJUDICE

Like the nation in which it resides, American baseball has a nasty history of segregation and discrimination. The major leagues have been integrated for sixty-one years (as of this writing); but for eighty years prior to Jackie Robinson's first game with the National League's Brooklyn Dodgers in 1947, black and white players played in separate (and not-so-equal) leagues.[9] While this separation remains a stain on the history of American sport and distorts the metrics we use to judge a player's greatness—keeping some of the nation's best players out of the majors gave the top players of that age an opportunity to pad their statistics against less talented pitchers and hitters,[10] and all-time greats such as Josh Gibson and Satchel Paige are not judged alongside other all-time greats—baseball is to be commended for exorcising the demons of black-white apartheid long before most American institutions, and certainly before the federal government. The Supreme Court handed down *Brown v. the Topeka Board of Education* in 1954, seven years after Jackie's first major league game; the "Little Rock Nine" enrolled in previously all-white Central High School an entire decade after baseball decided to integrate; the National Voting Rights Act didn't come around until 1965. By that time, Jackie Robinson—with the overwhelming support of his friends and teammates—had won the National League Rookie of the Year, the MVP award, and a World Series ring, and had been elected to the Baseball Hall of Fame. According to scholar and writer Henry Louis Gates Jr., sports in general took on special significance in the African American community during the twentieth century precisely because it "turned out to be one of the early conduits through which African Americans could integrate afield within the larger American society."[11]

Lest baseball get too much credit for being progressive in the realm of race relations, I have to point out that it would be another twelve years before each of the sixteen major league teams at the time had signed an African American player. (Three months after Robinson's first game, Larry Doby of the Cleveland Indians became the first black player in the American League. The Boston Red Sox were the last team to cross the color line, signing Pumpsie Green in 1959.) Still, sports became the nearly ideal venue for addressing prejudice. A player's performance on the field could in many cases supersede a fan's racial biases. Some prejudiced Dodgers fans were no doubt able to look past Jackie Robinson's race each time the All-Star second baseman stole home plate in spectacular fashion.

A NEW AGE IN AMERICAN SPORTS

Throughout the twentieth century, the world of sports continually challenged Americans' perceptions of race and racial differences. Jim Thorpe, a multisport athlete considered by many the greatest athlete of the first half of the twentieth century, often was the subject of stereotyping because of his Native American heritage.

African American boxer Joe Louis became a hero for many Americans, black and white, nearly two decades prior to the birth of the civil rights movement. Maya Angelou, in *I Know Why the Caged Bird Sings*, recalls listening to Louis's landmark victory over former heavyweight champion Primo Carnera in 1935: "Champion of the world. A Black boy. Some Black mother's son. He was the strongest man in the world. People drank Coca-Colas like ambrosia and ate candy bars like Christmas."[12]

Angelou also remembers Louis's victory being bittersweet: "It wouldn't do for a Black man and his family to be caught on a lonely country road on a night when Joe Louis had proved that we were the strongest people in the world."[13]

Another icon of the 1930s, Jesse Owens, famously won four gold medals at the 1936 "Nazi Olympics" in Berlin, shattering Adolph Hitler's theory of Aryan superiority as the chancellor watched from the stands. The events that Owens won—the 100 meter dash, the 200 meter dash, the long jump, and the 4 x 100 relay—left no doubt about his athletic prowess. He clearly ran faster and jumped farther than all the other athletes in the world, regardless of race. While his athletic abilities made Owens a national and global hero, he was nonetheless a victim of American segregation every time he left the stadium. As a student at Ohio State University, Owens, along with the school's other African American athletes, had to live off campus. He often had to sleep and eat away from his teammates, in "blacks only" hotels and restaurants. He returned from the Olympics to prejudice in his home country.[14]

> Although he received a New York ticker tape parade, he was forced to ride in a freight elevator to a reception in his honor at the Waldorf Astoria.
>
> "Although I wasn't invited to shake hands with Hitler," he said, "I wasn't invited to the White House to shake hands with the President, either."
>
> He failed to attract the endorsements and sponsorship deals enjoyed by white athletes and was reduced to running exhibition races against dogs and horses to make ends meet.[15]

Owens eventually was able to make a living from speaking engagements. Finally, in 1976—forty years after Owens's all-time great Olympic performance—President Gerald Ford awarded Owens the Medal of Freedom.[16]

While Jesse Owens was winning Olympic medals, John McClendon was a student at the University of Kansas. He had chosen to attend the school even though he was not allowed to play on the school's basketball team. McClendon was a skilled athlete, and basketball was his favorite sport. He was also an African American in Kansas in the 1930s. Though McClendon may have been able to play elsewhere, he enrolled at Kansas in hopes of learning from the school's head basketball coach, Dr. James Naismith. Naismith, of course, is best known for having invented the game of basketball in Springfield, Massachusetts, in 1891. Despite the school's restrictions on black athletes, Naismith agreed to mentor McClendon and taught him an up-tempo style of play in which players ran quickly up and down the court, playing from baseline to baseline. This was a departure from the half-court style of play that was common at major white colleges at the time. After leaving Kansas, Naismith's apprentice took a job as the head basketball coach at a small, historically black college in North Carolina, where he would institute Naismith's full-court style of play.

On a Sunday morning in 1944, the basketball team from Duke University and McClendon's team from the North Carolina College for

Negroes (which would in 1969 become North Carolina Central University) met at the YMCA in Durham, North Carolina, to play a secret and illegal basketball game. Both teams claimed to be the best team in North Carolina, and both teams had a legitimate claim to that title. Sadly, segregation laws kept them from facing off to determine which team was truly the best in the state. Playing an illegal game was the only way to find out. The two teams played at 11:00 in the morning, during church hour, and allowed no spectators in the gymnasium. The game remained a secret for several decades, known only to the players, coaches, and referees who had been present. McClendon's team won 88–44.[17] (More than thirty years later, the Duke team that advanced to the finals of the 1978 NCAA Tournament featured a style of play that was very similar to the style that McClendon had taught at North Carolina College for Negroes. Analysts praised Duke's uptempo offensive assault. But this praise did not sit well with McClendon disciple Ben Jobe. Jobe, a successful player and coach in his own right, said bitterly, "When Duke did it, it was genius. When we did it, it was jungle ball.")[18]

For many years, college sports were segregated in the same way that colleges themselves were segregated. African American players were largely limited to historically black colleges. While such schools themselves were products of segregation, they were responsible for equipping and empowering several generations of African American leaders and providing African American students a refuge from a racist and segregated society. Sports, and particularly basketball, at historically black colleges became very popular in the first half of the twentieth century. While the level of play at these schools was at least as good as, and likely better than, that of largely white teams, for many years black college teams had no recourse for showcasing their abilities outside of the African American community. Black schools were not allowed to participate in the most prestigious college basketball tournaments. In the 1940s and early 1950s the NCAA, NIT (National Invitational Tournament), and NAIB (National Association of Intercollegiate Basketball) (now NAIA, National Association of Intercollegiate Athletics) tournaments invited white teams only. In 1946 Indiana State University coach John Wooden, who would later win ten NCAA championships at UCLA, refused an NAIB tournament bid because his team's one black player would not be allowed to participate.[19] John McClendon tried unsuccessfully in 1948 to petition the NCAA to include black college teams. Eventually, in 1953, the NAIA accepted historically black institutions. Even then, the NAIA allowed only one black team to play in its postseason tournament.[20] African American schools met in a separate playoff to determine which team would get the tournament bid.

In 1950 the Washington Capitols in the NBA drafted the first two African American players in league history, Harold Hunter and Earl Lloyd Jr,, though Hunter was cut before playing a game. Yet the NBA was far from being integrated. For several years, no NBA team would sign more than one or two black players. Many of the best African American players played professionally in the Eastern Professional Basketball League. It would take the Supreme Court ruling in *Brown v. Board of Education* in Topeka to bring about true integration in basketball. After that ruling, some of the best African American players, including Oscar Robertson and Wilt Chamberlain, decided to attend historically white schools (Cincinnati for Robertson and Kansas for Chamberlain). Black players were gaining acceptance in the NBA. But the landmark moment for integration in basketball would come in 1966.

When Don Haskins arrived at Texas Western University in El Paso in 1961, he inherited a program that had already been integrated. At the time, integration at many schools meant having one or two African American players. Haskins decided that he would recruit the best players he could find, regardless of race. By the 1965–1966 season Haskins's Texas Western Miners team had an all-black starting lineup. That season the Miners put together a 23–1 record and advanced to the final game of the NCAA Tournament, where they met an all-white Kentucky team. Kentucky, at the time the most accomplished program in college basketball history, was widely favored to win the game. But the Texas Western squad—the first team ever to start five African American players in an NCAA championship game—upset Kentucky 72–65. In 1967 Vanderbilt's Perry Wallace became the first African American player in the previously all-white Southeastern Conference (Kentucky's conference). By the end of the decade Kentucky had signed its first African American player. Today, no one thinks twice about a team starting an all-black lineup.

Integration brought about a new age in American sports. After years of playing in separate leagues and tournaments the best players and teams could now compete with and against one another. Moreover, the success of athletes such as Jackie Robinson and Roberto Clemente gave young athletes hope of playing in the big leagues. For example, Althea Gibson, who overcame segregation to become the first African American to win a Grand Slam tennis tournament (in all she won five Grand Slam singles titles and six doubles), has been named as an inspiration by subsequent African American tennis greats such as Arthur Ashe, Zina Garrison, and Venus and Serena Williams. Ashe said, "I would not have had the chance to do what I have been able to do if Althea Gibson had not blazed the way for me."[21]

THE SCOREBOARD IS COLOR-BLIND

Clearly racism and prejudice have haunted sports much as they have haunted other facets of American life. And sports have continued to struggle with these demons long after Joe Louis won the heavyweight title or Jackie Robinson broke baseball's color barrier. There are still broadcasters and analysts who seem to automatically assume that a black player's success is due to pure athletic talent and a white player's success is due to hard work and determination.[22] The fact is that to succeed at the highest levels of sport one must be blessed with natural ability *and* work hard in practice and during the off season. Interiorizing and applying these assumptions may take several more years.

But sports also have a natural means of confronting prejudice: fair and objective competition. Sure, there always have been and always will be referees, umpires, and officials in every sport with hidden (or in rare instances overt) biases. And the outcome of contests in sports such as diving, gymnastics, and figure skating hinges on the decisions of necessarily subjective judges. But often in sports the winner is simply and clearly the athlete with the fastest time or the team that has scored the most goals. Clocks and scoreboards tend to be color-blind.

In athletic competition, many of these factors that divide us are rendered meaningless. Whether a player earns a spot on an NBA roster has little to do with whether he comes from Chicago, California, Croatia, or China but, rather, with his size, speed, ball-handling skill, court vision, and jump shot.[23] The ability to throw a change-up or hit a ball over the right field wall has nothing to do with race or nationality. Thus professional baseball and basketball especially have become bastions of diversity, boasting star players from several nations. The success of many teams in these leagues demonstrates that ethnic, racial, and cultural diversity contributes to and does not hinder corporate success.

Consider, for example, the San Antonio Spurs, a franchise that won four NBA championships between 1999 and 2007 and made the playoffs every year in between. During three of the team's four playoff runs, the Spurs were led by the trio of Tim Duncan, Manu Ginobili, and Tony Parker. Duncan hails from the U.S. Virgin Islands, Ginobili is from Argentina (and was the MVP of the 2004 Olympic basketball tournament in which Argentina won the gold medal), and Parker is French. Duncan played four years at Wake Forest University; Ginobili played several seasons in South America and Europe before playing for the Spurs; Parker crossed the pond to play in the NBA as soon as he was eligible. Duncan is black; Ginobili is white; Parker has an African American father and a white European mother. These differences are inconsequential on the court. Together the trio, along with a diverse cast of teammates, has become one of the most reliable teams in pro sports.

More than sixty years after Jackie Robinson broke baseball's color barrier, most fans and people who are involved in sports know that they cannot judge an athlete based on race, ethnicity, nationality, or cultural heritage. Athletes of all races and backgrounds have been successful in many sports at many levels through a combination of hard work, passion, knowledge of their sport, and natural ability.

"NO LONGER JEW NOR GREEK"

One might compare integration in sports to the early church's mission to the Gentiles. The analogy is far from perfect: Gentiles, for example, were not second-class citizens in the Roman world the way blacks were second-class citizens under American segregation; outside of the synagogue or regions with large Jewish populations, such as Galilee and Judea, the name "Gentile" would have been meaningless. And the barriers that separated Jewish and Gentile Christians were grounded in ancient religious traditions rather than racial prejudices. Still, both Gentile Christians and minority ballplayers struggled to gain acceptance from a reluctant establishment.

The early church's mission to those outside of the house of Israel has its roots in Old Testament books such as Ruth and Jonah. In Ruth the hero and title character is a Moabite. Moab historically was an enemy of Israel, and Israelite tradition held that the Moabites were descendants of an incestuous relationship (see Gen. 19:32–38). Ruth marries the son of Naomi, an Israelite widow. When Naomi's sons die, she decides to return to Judah in Israel and urges her Moabite daughters-in-law to stay behind and take new husbands. But Ruth refuses to leave Naomi, saying, "Where you go, I will go; where you lodge, I will lodge; your people shall be my people, and your God my God" (Ruth 1:16b). Ruth follows Naomi to Judah, where she takes a husband, Boaz, and becomes the great-grandmother of David, Israel's most beloved king and the father of a great dynasty in Jerusalem (Ruth 4:18–22). Despite tensions between Israel and Moab, tradition held that King David himself had Moabite blood. Coaches and executives in once predominantly white major college and professional sports eventually had to acknowledge the contributions of African American (as well as Hispanic, Asian American, and Native American) players and coaches. Likewise, Israel had to acknowledge that even a Moabite could make an important contribution to the history of their great nation.

The book of Jonah tells the story of a prophet, Jonah, called to preach a message of doom to the people of Nineveh: God will hold them accountable for their wickedness. Nineveh was the capital of the Assyrian Empire, which would destroy the northern kingdom of Israel toward the end of the eighth century, B.C.E. After being sidetracked (and swallowed by a fish), Jonah proclaims to the Ninevites the destruction that is upon them, at which point the people of Nineveh repent of their sin. When Nineveh repents, God relents, much to Jonah's chagrin. Jonah cannot understand why God would spare such a wicked city. But God is not interested in Jonah's grudges or prejudices; God sees the Ninevites' repentance as an opportunity to redeem a city that had gone astray. The sports world has no wicked cities (though several people in Ann Arbor would identify Columbus, Ohio, as such, and vice versa), but we see examples throughout the twentieth and into the twenty-first century of people overcoming prejudices and welcoming new players and coaches into the fold.

The early church's ministry to the Gentiles begins with the ministry of Jesus himself. In Mark's Gospel, while Jesus is traveling through the bustling Phoenician seaport of Tyre, a local woman—described as a Gentile and Syrophoenician—accosts him and begs him to cast a demon out of her daughter. Jesus's response to the woman is disturbing on its surface. He says to her, "Let the children be fed first, for it is not fair to take the children's food and throw it to the dogs" (Mark 7:27). The children to whom Jesus refers are the Jewish people—the children of Israel. "Dogs" is a derogatory term for Gentiles. Jesus intimates that only Jews, and not Gentiles, are worthy of his ministry of healing and reconciliation. But the Syrophoenician woman doesn't accept his answer. She will not accept that she is unworthy of Jesus's healing touch, even if she is a "dog." She answers, "Sir, even the dogs under the table eat the children's crumbs" (Mark 7:28). Impressed by her faith, her courage, or her quick wit, Jesus responds by healing the woman's daughter. Suddenly, this unnamed Gentile woman goes from being a dog to being a person of faith worthy of compassion and healing.

A similar story in John's Gospel tells about Jesus's meeting with a Samaritan woman at a well (John 4:1-42). Jews and Samaritans claim a common heritage, but disputes about this heritage and fundamental differences in worship practices were cause for animosity between the two groups in the first century. Despite this tension, Jesus approaches the Samaritan woman and asks her for a drink of water. This simple request leads to a conversation about "living water" and the woman's marital status. Eventually, the Samaritan woman brings up the chief cultural difference that makes her conversation with Jesus so unlikely in the first place. She says, "Our ancestors worshiped on this mountain, but you say that the place where people must worship is in Jerusalem" (John 4:20). Jesus responds by saying that this distinction, which had separated their ancestors for centuries, is now moot. His disciples are shocked that Jesus is talking to a woman, let alone a Samaritan woman, but Jesus is less concerned with the woman's gender and ethnicity than with her potential to contribute to his mission. Because of the woman's testimony, many Samaritans become Jesus's followers (John 4:39).

The Samaritan woman was not the only one of Jesus's friends whom his closest disciples had reservations about. In Mark and Luke the disciple John objects to an outsider casting out demons in Jesus's name. Jesus says to John, "Whoever is not against us is for us" (Mark 9:38–41; see also Luke 9:49–50). As the early church developed in the decades following Easter and Pentecost, Jesus's Jewish followers' attitude toward Gentiles evolved. We see this new attitude at work in Philip's Bible study with the Ethiopian eunuch (Acts 8:26–40), in Peter's vision of unclean animals that God had declared clean and his subsequent instruction to minister to a God-fearing Gentile named Cornelius (Acts 10:1–33), and in the decision by the Council of Jerusalem to exempt Gentile Christians from much of the Mosaic law (Acts 15:1–21). In each case the apostles focused on the potential contributions of Gentile Christians rather than on reasons to exclude these new believers.

Throughout his letters to young churches, Paul rejects distinctions based on cultural and religious heritage, social status, and gender. He wrote to the fledgling churches in Galatia in Asia Minor, "There is no longer Jew or Greek, there is no longer slave or free, there is no longer male and female; for all of you are one in Christ Jesus. And if you belong to Christ, then you are Abraham's offspring, heirs according to the promise" (Gal.s 3:28–29; see also 1 Cor. 12:13 and Col. 3:11).

"THE MOST SEGREGATED MAJOR INSTITUTION IN AMERICA"

Cynics, like those who were critical of Branch Rickey, might argue that many of the white coaches and executive who were responsible for giving African American athletes opportunities to play major college and professional sports did so not in the interest of justice but in the interest of gaining a competitive edge. By allowing black players on their rosters, they were widening the circle of talent from which they could draw; they gave themselves access to skilled players that their competitors had declared unacceptable. Although such an attitude seems, on its surface, selfish, it gets at what Jesus meant when he told his disciples that those who were not against them were for them. Anyone who is willing to use his or her gifts to achieve a common goal should be welcomed into the community.

Advocating for Gentiles to join the church as Gentiles—rather than as Jewish converts—fit Paul's understanding of Jewish eschatology. New Testament scholar Amy-Jill Levine writes,

> [Paul] knew that the God of Israel was also the God of the Gentiles and that the Gentiles, qua Gentiles, would accept this theological truth in the last days. In other words, for Paul, the Gentiles would come into the messianic realm as Gentiles; they did not have to be Jews in order to be in right relationship with God.[24]

Paul also believed that a new age—the messianic age—had begun and pointed to the church's successful mission to the Gentiles as proof. Much as the full inclusion of African American and other minority athletes in the top professional leagues and college programs signified a new age in American sports, the full inclusion of Gentiles in the body of Christ was evidence that God was doing something new and great.

But nearly two millennia after Paul wrote his message of impartiality and inclusion, the church is still learning its lesson. In 1963 Dr. Martin Luther King Jr. famously remarked, "We must face the fact that in America, the church is still the most segregated major institution in America. At 11:00 on Sunday morning when we stand and sing and Christ has no east or west, we stand at the most segregated hour in this nation."[25] Most Christian traditions have, at some point in their history, struggled with the demons of prejudice and exclusion, and many still do. According to the United Methodist Church's 2008 State of the Church Report, 71 percent of clergy and 66 percent of laity still feel that it is extremely important for their denomination to focus on ending racial division in the church.[26] While several congregations have made progress in this regard, many others remain largely homogeneous. Continued segregation in the sanctuary is in part voluntary, the result of differences in language and culture that have an impact on the worship experience. Nonetheless, the church can do much more to integrate the pews. Congregations can identify and confront any prejudices or other barriers that prevent them from being welcoming to all people. The church can also strive for diversity in leadership, both at the congregational level and at the conference, diocese, district, or presbytery level.

In this regard Christians today can still learn much from the enormous strides toward equality that were taken in major college and professional sports during the twentieth century. When people are left out, their contributions and example also are left out, and we fall short of God's will. When all are welcome and treated with dignity and encouraged to contribute, the church benefits from the gifts and witness of people with a wide range of life experiences. and those on the outside can look at the church and say, "I would be welcomed there. I belong there." We have seen how integration and diversity have transformed the world of sports; the church will reap similar rewards as it continues making progress toward being more inclusive and diverse.

4

"EQUAL WORTH IN THE EYES OF GOD"[1]

The Apostle Paul, Billie Jean King, and the Issue of Gender

[Women] get 8% of the sports page. We have about
$1 billion in sponsorship worldwide—men have more than $25 billion.
And that's just the beginning.

—BILLIE JEAN KING

On the seventh day, when the king was merry with wine,
he commanded . . . the seven eunuchs who attended him,
to bring Queen Vashti before the king, wearing the royal crown,
in order to show the peoples and the officials her beauty;
for she was fair to behold. But Queen Vashti
refused to come at the king's command.

—ESTHER 1:10–12

My high school was a girls' basketball school. During my junior and senior seasons the Perry Meridian High School Lady Falcons were one of the best teams in Indiana. Attendance at girls' basketball games rivaled that of football and boys' basketball games, even though most of the girls' games were played on weekdays instead of on Friday nights.

For the students and community members who packed the gym to watch the Falcons swoop down and devour their competition, gender was a nonissue. We had a great team with great players; it didn't matter whether they were girls or boys. On the other hand, had our girls' basketball team not been one of the better teams in the state (and had our boys' basketball team been more successful), most in the student body and the community likely would have ignored the sport, much as they ignored other sports that weren't football or boys basketball. We were progressive when it came to gender in sports, but we had a reason to be.

In Galatians 3:28 Paul writes, "There is no longer Jew or Greek, there is no longer slave or free, there is no longer *male and female;* for all of you are one in Christ Jesus" (emphasis mine). Though the sports world should be commended on the progress it has made in the areas of race relations and cultural issues, an enormous gender gap persists in athletics—and in the church.

In part, this gap is physiological. Men and women are different. And while I can think of hundreds of women off the top of my head who could run faster than me, jump higher than me, and throw a ball with more precision than I can, generally speaking the best male athletes are bigger, faster, and stronger than the best female athletes. Thus men's sports tend to attract more viewers and more money.

Yet while male and female athletes differ physiologically, they do not differ significantly when it comes to desire, drive, commitment, and competitiveness. Anyone who watches both men's and women's sports knows that an athlete's passion for the game has nothing to do with gender. In tennis and in some Olympic sports, such as swimming and gymnastics, the popularity of the women's game rivals that of the men's. In many other sports this is not the case. The national love of soccer in many European, African, and Latin American nations largely does not extend to the women's game. While women's basketball has steadily gained popularity in the United States, the WNBA has struggled in terms of attendance and television ratings and remains a common target for sports columnists who are critical of the level of play and quick to point out the less-than-stellar ratings and attendance figures. (Sadly, during the writing of this book the WNBA suspended operation of its most storied franchise, the Houston Comets. The Comets won the first four WNBA titles in the late 1990s with all-time-great players such as Cynthia Cooper and Sheryl Swoopes.)

Complete gender equality across all sports may not be possible, but the sports world would do well to continue taking steps in that direction. Of course, several important steps have already been taken. Tennis great Billie Jean King fought hard for equal prize money in her sport's biggest tournaments. Thanks in large part to her efforts the U.S. Open began awarding the same prize money to its men's and women's champions in 1973. Wimbledon finally came on board in 2007. King also defeated Bobby Riggs, formerly the top-ranked men's player in the world, in 1973's infamous "Battle of the Sexes" in Houston's Astrodome. (For more on that match, see chapter 2.) During the 1999 FIFA Women's World Cup the United States' women's soccer team sold out the ninety-thousand-seat Rose Bowl for its championship win over China. Players such as Mia Hamm and Brandi Chastain (who famously tore off her jersey, revealing a sports bra, after scoring the game-winning shootout goal) became household names. In the 1970s Janet Guthrie became the first woman to race in NASCAR's Winston Cup (now the Sprint Cup) and to qualify for the Indianapolis 500; in 2008 Danica Patrick won the Indy Japan 300, making her the first woman to win a race in a major auto racing series.

Perhaps the most significant step toward gender equality in sports has been Title IX of the Education Amendments of 1972. Title IX urges equality in ten key educational areas, including access to higher education and math and science education, but is best known for its effects on high school and college athletics. Title IX mandates equal opportunity for male and female athletes. The website TitleIX.info reminds readers that, prior to Title IX, very few girls participated in high school sports and there were "virtually no college scholarships for female athletes."[2] Since Title IX opportunities for girls and women in sports have increased at all levels. The best female athletes, like their male counterparts, now have access to professional coaches and world-class facilities. TitleIX.info also points out the health benefits for women who participate in sports: "They're less likely to smoke, drink, use drugs and experience unwanted pregnancies. Studies also link sports participation to reduced incidences of breast cancer and osteoporosis later in life."[3]

Despite the efforts of pioneers such as King and the positive effects of Title IX, female athletes still have a long way to go to achieve equality with their male peers. As King points out, "[W]e get 8% of the sports page. We have about $1 billion in sponsorship worldwide—men have more than $25 billion. And that's just the beginning."[4]

Adding another layer of complexity to the problem of gender inequality in sports is the sexual objectification of some female athletes. During the late 1990s and the early years of the twenty-first century, Russian tennis star Anna Kournikova was one of the world's most popular athletes despite the fact that she never won a professional singles tournament. (In Kournikova's defense, she has won several women's doubles titles, often with former world number one Martina Hingis as a partner.) Early in her career Kournikova showed promise, but her popularity was largely due to her being a sex symbol. She appeared scantily clad in several men's magazines and in provocative ads for a sport bra line. Several players ranked ahead of Kournikova remained relative unknowns, even among tennis fans. Kournikova's popularity slowly waned as her world ranking dropped and she continually lost in the early rounds of major tournaments. Scores of Kournikova fan websites, many of which feature racy photos of the tennis pro, are still active on the Internet.

When Maria Sharapova won Wimbledon in 2004, many were quick to draw comparisons between her and Anna Kournikova. Like Kournikova, Sharapova was tall, blond, and pretty; like Kournikova, Sharapova's fan base included people who were drawn to her more for her looks than for her tennis skills. (The fact that both women are Russian and have names ending in the common suffix "ova" only fueled the comparisons.) But Sharapova, unlike Kournikova, had won a title— arguably the biggest title in tennis. And she has continued to be one of the top-ranked players in the world and has several singles titles, including a few majors, to her credit. Sharapova is a bona fide tennis star who has done more than enough to have earned not being relegated to sex-symbol status. Sadly (in my opinion) Sharapova has nonetheless participated in her share of racy photo shoots.

Olympic swimmer Amanda Beard was another successful athlete-turned-sex symbol. Beard posed nude for *Playboy* following the 2004

Olympics. In 2008, CNN.com ran a headline that referred to Beard as a "nude pin-up swimmer." Beard had won seven medals in three Olympic games, yet a major news organization decided that she would best be described as a "nude pin-up."

In a 2007 *Sports Illustrated* article by Aditi Kinkhabwala, Mary Jo Kane, director of the University of Minnesota's Tucker Center for Research of Girls and Women in Sport lamented that female athletes have historically been "portrayed in ways that emphasize 'femininity and sexualization over athletic competence.'"[5] The article goes on to say that:

> Females across the board are drawn to images of athletic competence. So are men, in the 35 to 55 age range, who think of their daughters. "They don't see," Kane said, "how a passive, sexualized pose is celebrating an athletic body. How do bare breasts increase respect for and interest in women sports?"[6]

While Kinkhabwala's article adeptly explained the problem of the sexualization of female athletes, others at *Sports Illustrated* missed the point. When the story first appeared on the magazine's website, readers could click on links to see sexy photos of Beard and Sharapova from the magazine's Swimsuit Collection.[7]

The sexualization of the female athlete is not a failure of the male-dominated sports business so much as it is a response to a culture in which sex sells, sometimes to the tune of millions of dollars. Racy images of attractive female celebrities, including athletes, sell magazines, drive traffic to websites, and draw attention to products. (I understand that this also applies to male athletes, albeit to a lesser degree. A shirtless LeBron James doesn't hurt magazine sales.) For female athletes who, on the whole, are paid less and are less recognizable than their male counterparts, marketing themselves as sex symbols is an effective way to gain notoriety and to make more money than they could earn simply by playing in tournaments. In 2001, for instance, Lisa Harrison, a relatively unknown WNBA player, became one of the most searched-for athletes on the Internet after announcing that she would *consider* posing for *Playboy*.[8] Harrison refused an offer to pose that reportedly would have paid her more than $500,000[9] (more than twelve times greater than her WNBA salary at the time.) Even stars such as Maria

Sharapova and Danica Patrick, who are marketable athletes in a tennis skirt and fire suit, respectively, have gained much financially by posing for pictures in a bikini.

There's plenty of money to be made from the sexualization of female athletes, but there's also a cost. In 2008 CNN Newsroom did an excellent story about a high school football team in South Carolina that had two girls on its varsity squad. Both were placekickers and both had put points on the board that season. CNN made the unfortunate decision to follow the story with another story about women in football and ran a piece on the Lingerie Football League, in which scantily clad models play a modified version of tackle football. I wrote at the time:

> Placing the stories back-to-back seemed to say, "Hey girls, in high school you can work hard to make it and earn the respect of your teammates in a sport where girls traditionally have not been welcome; then, a few years later, you can continue your football career by stripping down to your underwear so that depraved men can gawk at you."[10]

Famed radio personality Don Imus was far more explicit in his (racially tinged) objectification of female athletes when, following the 2007 NCAA women's basketball championship game between Tennessee and Rutgers, he said that the Tennessee players were cute and the Rutgers players were rough, referring to them as "nappy-headed ho's."[11] Due to public outcry Imus's radio show and its televised simulcast lost sponsors faster than Flo Jo ran the 100-meter dash, and Imus lost his job. (He has since secured a new radio gig.) Perhaps the reaction to Imus's comments was a stand against the objectification of female athletes (as well as against the casual use of racial epithets). At the very least, women athletes, like their male counterparts, deserve to be judged by the performance on the court, field, or track and not by their sex appeal. (To be fair, some male athletes also are praised for their good looks or derided for their lack thereof.)

Women in the church have faced struggles similar to those faced by women in sports. They have been denied opportunities; dismissed as less than their male counterparts; and, when given a chances to serve in positions of leadership, often have been judged by a different standard than men in the same positions. A fair and complete assessment of the role and place of women in the church is beyond the scope of this book, in part because it varies so much from one denomination or tradition to the next. Nonetheless, all Christians must acknowledge that, throughout Scripture, God places women in key leadership positions: Miriam is a prophet and worship leader (Exod. 15:20–21); Deborah is a judge and military leader (Judg. 4–5); the prophet Huldah plays a key role in King Josiah's reformation (2 Kings 22); Esther is a queen who saves her people from destruction (see chapter 8, "For Such a Time as This"); Mary gives birth to and raises God's anointed son; Mary Magdalene, Joanna, and Susanna bankroll Jesus's ministry (Luke 8:1–3); Paul refers to Phoebe as a deacon (Ro. 16:1) and names Junia as "prominent among the apostles" (Rom. 16:7). These are just a few of many examples.

The church must also name and reject ways in which women—whether in sports, entertainment, the workplace, or elsewhere—are objectified or exploited sexually. We must affirm that all human beings have been created by God as people of worth and dignity, that the human body is a "temple of the Holy Spirit" (1 Cor. 6:19) that should not be exploited, and that God does not look on one's "outward appearance" but on one's heart (1 Sam. 16:7). We can point to the example of Queen Vashti in the Book of Esther: When her husband, King Ahasuerus, asked her to show off her beauty to his banquet guests, Vashti refused, even though her refusal would cost Vashti her crown (Esth. 1:10–20).

Many traditions have taken long strides in this direction. The Social Principles of the United Methodist Church, for example, affirm that women and men have "equal worth in the eyes of God,"[12] that women have a right to "equal treatment in employment, responsibility, promotion, and compensation,"[13] and that it is important that women serve "in decision-making positions at all levels of Church life."[14] Several denominations have women serving at the highest level of ecclesial leadership, and women outnumber men in many mainline Protestant seminaries. Many church curriculum publishers are developing resources that help young people establish a healthy and positive self-image and respect for the human body so that they will be able to resist cultural messages that cheapen and exploit the body and sexuality.

Both the church and the world of sports have come a long way in the realm of equality for women, but both have a long way to go. Both institutions need to address sexism within and both have an opportunity to set an example for the larger society. The church can point to a long history, dating back to biblical times, of strong women called by God to be in positions of leadership and a scriptural mandate to treat the human body with honor and respect. The sports world can point to strong (literally and figuratively) women who have achieved success—in some cases in sports dominated by men—through commitment and perseverance. Influential coaches, players, and executives also could (and should) use their influence and notoriety to reject the sexualization of female athletes. Where gender is concerned, church and sport can grow together.

5

ONE BODY, MANY PARTS

Winning and Losing as a Team

The way a team plays as a whole determines its success.
You may have the greatest bunch of individual stars in the world,
but if they don't play together, the club won't be worth a dime.

—BABE RUTH

Now you are the body of Christ and
individually members of it.

—1 CORINTHIANS 12:27

BILL RUSSELL'S ONE DISAPPOINTING SEASON

By almost any measure Bill Russell was one of the greatest basketball players ever. He led the University of San Francisco Dons to two NCAA titles and a record of 57–1 during his junior and senior years. He won a gold medal with the 1956 Olympic team. His Celtics teams won the NBA title in eleven of his thirteen NBA seasons and advanced to the finals in twelve. Even his high school and summer travel teams were successful. John Wooden declared Russell the greatest defensive player he had ever seen.[1]

Bill Russell, by his own admission, had one major blemish on his record: his sophomore season at the University of San Francisco. He recalls this season in his autobiography *Second Wind*:

> We had wall-to-wall jerks on that team, and we couldn't win. I played my heart out, but our team was riddled with dissension, and I was part of it. I was not strong enough to change the atmosphere for the better, and the team wasn't strong enough to change me, so we feuded. There was bad feeling among almost all the players, so though everyone played well, we still lost. Sometimes I'm haunted by the thought that my whole career could have been like that one season if certain ingredients hadn't changed. Most of them had to do with the team.[2]

Many players would give a good portion of their salaries for the luxury of complaining about the one season when they were on a bad team, the one season in which their team didn't contend for a championship. Ted Williams, Dan Marino, Charles Barkley, and Karl Malone are among the all-time great players in their respective sports who never won a championship at the highest level. No one questions these players' desire and drive, and few would suggest that they were not team players. Yet their otherwise prestigious careers seem somehow incomplete because they never won a championship ring. Of course, hundreds of lesser players, most of whom will never be hall of famers, and many of whom sports history has forgotten, possess a gaudy ring with several diamonds and an inscription saying they were part of a championship team. Can you name the backup long snapper for the 1986 New York Giants? No? Well, he has a Super Bowl ring, and Dan Marino doesn't.

Although all major sports hand out a variety of individual awards—for the most valuable player, the best defensive player, the best first-year player, the most improved player, and so on—most basketball, football, soccer, baseball, softball, volleyball, and hockey players understand that individual achievements are secondary to the team's accomplishments. And the best team-sports athletes understand that every player on the team, even that backup long snapper, has a part to play in the team's success. In team sports the best player doesn't always win a championship, nor does the team with the best collection of talent, the most expensive rosters, or the highest rated recruiting classes. The championship goes to the best team.

NOT JUST A SET OF INDIVIDUAL PLAYERS

Indiana University's men's basketball season began the 2007–2008 season ranked in the top ten and stayed there for several weeks. But in early February the NCAA informed the school that coach Kelvin Sampson was guilty of major rules violations related to recruiting. The school immediately launched an internal investigation and, by the end of the month, Sampson had resigned. The uncertainty surrounding Sampson's fate and the shock the players felt following his resignation sent the team into turmoil. Despite having one of the nation's best rosters, the Hoosiers ended the regular season with seven losses and an eighth seed in the NCAA Tournament (a far cry from the second or third seed they had expected earlier in the season). Arkansas beat them handily in the first round of the tourney. The roster didn't change, nor did the talent of the players; but the team changed. The collective mood changed, as did the collective morale and sense of purpose. Early in the season, Indiana had achieved success as a team; late in the season, Indiana struggled as a team.

Conversely, the 1990 Loyola Marymount Lions were able to achieve incredible success as a team, even after tragically losing their best player. In March of 1990, a couple weeks before the beginning of the NCAA Tournament, Loyola's best player, Hank Gathers, collapsed during a game and died. Gathers suffered from a heart disorder. Losing Gathers left a hole in the Lions' lineup that would be nearly impossible to fill. After all, Gathers was the team's star player and emotional leader. But by suffering together through Gathers's untimely death, the Loyola Marymount players grew closer as a team. Led by Bo Kimble, Gathers's best friend and the Lions' other superstar, Loyola Marymount exceeded expectations by advancing to the regional finals (Elite Eight) of the NCAA Tournament before losing to the eventual champion, the University of Nevada, Las Vegas. During the team's tournament run, right-handed Kimble shot his first free throw of every game with his left hand in honor of Gathers, who had been left-handed. He never missed a left-handed free throw.

As a fan of the Tennessee Titans, I worried about how the team would perform after losing cornerback Adam "Pacman" Jones to a year-long suspension in 2007. His suspension was related to several off-the-field arrests and other incidents. Jones had been arguably the best player on a 2006 Titans team that had won eight of its final eleven games and seemed headed in the right direction after several years of missing the playoffs. Though Jones's disciplinary problems had been a distraction, his play on the field was at times stellar. Losing him for a season seemed to be taking a step backward. But it wasn't. In the absence of Pacman's antics, the team came together and in 2007 improved to 10–6 and earned a playoff spot. The Titans finished the 2008 season 13–3, with the best record in the NFL; Jones took his off-the-field drama to Dallas, which cut him at the end of the 2008 season.

The point is that a team is not just a set of individual players. A team's ability cannot be determined by taking the sum of the abilities of the team's players. Talented players are only valuable when their talents complement those of their teammates.

Judy Marra Martelli, who played on the Immaculata College teams that won three women's basketball national championships in the early 1970s (and who is married to St. Joseph's University men's basketball coach Phil Martelli), attributes her team's success to the fact that "chemistry was evident among the players" and that their desire to play focused on team, and not individual, accomplishments.

Bill Russell attributes the success of his 1960s Celtics teams to players being willing to play a certain role, even if a role did not make full use of an individual player's gifts:

> Professional athletes, being competitive and vain, usually find it difficult to accept limited roles, but the Celtics were wise enough to know how important it is. Sam [Jones] and K.C. Jones [no relation] knew for certainty that neither one of them would ever start as long as [Bob] Cousy and [Bill] Sharman played, but they accepted their roles because we were winning. Similarly, Frank Ramsey and John Havlicek were better players

than various Celtics who started ahead of them, but neither of them fussed. Instead, they made the "sixth man" part of the language of basketball.[3]

If one is truly invested in the success of his or her team, he or she will be willing to sacrifice individual statistics and accolades in the interest of winning. Teammates must unite around a common purpose for the team to be successful.

BODY PARTS

The Apostle Paul wrote to the church in Corinth about the importance of functioning as a team. And like Bill Russell, Paul emphasizes the importance of knowing and embracing one's role:

> For just as the body is one and has many members, and all the members of the body, though many, are one body, so it is with Christ. For in the one Spirit we were all baptized into one body—Jews or Greeks, slaves or free—and we were all made to drink of one Spirit.
>
> Indeed, the body does not consist of one member but of many. If the foot were to say, "Because I am not a hand, I do not belong to the body," that would not make it any less a part of the body. And if the ear were to say, "Because I am not an eye, I do not belong to the body," that would not make it any less a part of the body. If the whole body were an eye, where would the hearing be? If the whole body were hearing, where would the sense of smell be? (1 Cor. 12:12–17)

A successful team in any sport operates according to the same principles as the body of Christ, but the metaphor applies most clearly to football. Certain positions on the field—such as quarterback, wide receiver, running back, and cornerback—are more glamorous than others. Quick, make a list of every current NFL quarterback you can think of. Now list every current NFL offensive tackle you can think of. Chances are your quarterback list is much longer even though offensive tackles outnumber quarterbacks on most rosters. But while a right guard on the offensive line or a blocker on the kick-return team isn't likely to win a

Heisman Trophy or be the NFL's Most Valuable Player, these positions are nonetheless essential to the team's success. As of this writing, only one pure placekicker and no pure punters have been enshrined in the Pro Football Hall of Fame.[4] Yet no team has made the playoffs or won a Super Bowl without a kicker and punter, and on more than one occasion a last-minute field goal attempt has determined the Super Bowl's outcome.[5] Every player—on offense, defense, special teams, and even the practice squad—is an important part of the body. Just as the human body needs its pancreas, the football team needs its long snapper.

The role that one plays in the body of Christ, much like the position that one plays on a team, depends on one's gifts. Paul acknowledges that some roles within the church are more glamorous than others: "God has appointed in the church first apostles, second prophets, third teachers; then deeds of power, then gifts of healing, forms of assistance, forms of leadership, various kinds of tongues" (1 Cor. 12:28). When the body or the team is at its best, the people in the most glamorous positions (whether quarterback or bishop or team captain or prophet) are the people whose gifts are best suited to those positions. The healthy church or team assigns positions of prestige by discerning who has the gifts that are necessary for that role, not by using criteria such as tenure or popularity. Yet the most prestigious roles are not necessarily the most valuable. Healthy teams and churches also celebrate the contributions of members in less prestigious positions whose contributions are nonetheless essential to the well-being of the entire body. The second-string left tackle and the church bus driver need to know that their roles and contributions are important and valued.

One of the surest signs that a team is dysfunctional is players blaming their teammates for the team's struggles. This type of dysfunction always has an adverse effect on team performance. It is especially common in football, where different players are often responsible for the offense and the defense. If a team loses by a score of 7–6, the defensive players who allowed only one touchdown may be inclined to lash out at the offense's inability to put more points on the board. Similarly, if a team loses by a score of 49–38, a productive offensive unit may express frustration with a defense that gave up so many points.

In other sports, such division may result when one player feels as though he or she must carry the team on his or her back. In 2001, NBA All-Star Stephon Marbury, then of the New Jersey Nets, wrote the words "all alone" on his shoe, a not-so-subtle jab at teammate Keith Van Horn, the team's other star, whom Marbury felt was not pulling his weight. Many church families have suffered when members, clergy, or staff people have been inclined to blame their brothers and sisters in Christ for the congregation's struggles. Similarly, dysfunction results when a player takes too much credit for his or her team's success or when a pastor takes too much credit for a surge of members who are actively engaged in the life of his or her congregation. For his part, Paul affirms the old coaching cliché, "We win as a team; we lose as a team," saying, "If one member [of the body] suffers, all suffer together; if one member is honored, all rejoice together with it" (1 Cor. 12:26; see also Rom. 12:15).

Being a good teammate requires humility. It requires one to acknowledge and celebrate the gifts and contributions of one's teammates, and it requires one to put the success and well-being of the team before individual goals. In auto racing the trophies are awarded to individuals, but those close to the sport understand that racing is a team game. A good pit crew can save a driver valuable seconds that may ultimately determine whether he or she wins a race. The crew chief acts as a coach and helps make important decisions about driving strategy and when a driver should make a pit stop. In auto racing, most members of the team anonymously work together for the glory of the driver. Cycling is another "individual" sport in which teamwork is instrumental to success. On many cycling teams, most members are not expected to try to win races. Instead, they are expected to help their team leader win by reining in breakaway competitors and allowing the team leader to ride directly behind them and conserve energy by drafting.

John the Baptist explained that, though he had substantial influence and a sizable following, he was only an advance messenger whose job was to "prepare the way" (Mark 1:3) of one who would be much greater. In the fourth Gospel, John tells his audience, "[Jesus] must increase, but I must decrease" (John 3:30). When Jesus's disciples argued about which of them was the greatest, Jesus said, "Whoever wants to be first must be last of all and servant of all" (Mark 9:35). Mary's Magnificat in Luke anticipates Jesus's maxim that those "who are first will be last, and the last will be first" (Mark 10:31):

> *He has brought down the powerful from their thrones,*
> *and lifted up the lowly;*
> *he has filled the hungry with good things,*
> *and sent the rich away empty. (Luke 1:52–53)*

God calls us not to seek individual gain or glory but to humble ourselves for the good of the team, the body of Christ, and all of God's creation.

THE MINISTRY OF ALL BELIEVERS

Perhaps sports teams give the church an illustration of the ministry or priesthood of all believers—the belief, popularized by Martin Luther, that God calls all people to be ministers of the gospel. A baseball team includes pitchers (left- and right-handed starters, middle relievers, and a closer), catchers, infielders (first, second, and third basemen and shortstops), outfielders (left, right, and center fielders), and (except in the National League) designated hitters; yet all are baseball players. A football team includes offensive, defensive, and special teams players, skill players and linemen, players who play multiple positions and players who specialize; but all are football players. The church includes prophets, preachers, Sunday school teachers, program directors, childcare providers, custodians, and missionaries; yet all are ministers.

And, as Paul reminds us, no minister—whether a worship leader, a food bank volunteer, or a committee chair—operates in a vacuum. Each is part of the body and must work in concert with other body parts. A running back cannot be effective without the help of a strong offensive line; and a youth minister cannot be effective without the help of a team of parents and other adults who are willing to give of their time and gifts. A center in basketball will be limited offensively without a good point guard who can get her the ball; and a missionary will be limited without the support of those who fund, organize, and assist in her mission work. Every athlete needs teammates who will support him and hold him accountable; every Christians needs spiritual friends and mentors who will support him and hold him accountable.

Ministers need to be aware not only of the people whose support they rely on but also people who rely on their support. If a football or basketball or soccer player is poorly conditioned, his or her lack of preparation will have an adverse effect on the entire team. If a player acts selfishly and decides to focus on individual statistics instead of whether the team wins, the team's performance will suffer. Likewise, if a member of the church neglects or refuses to use his or her spiritual gifts for the good of the church, opportunities for ministry may be lost. If a disgruntled player, upset about playing time or a coaching decision, refuses to support his or her teammates, the team's chemistry will suffer. If a church member, out of apathy or spite, refuses to support a ministry of the congregation, that ministry will not achieve its full potential.

CHRISTIANITY IS A TEAM SPORT

Christianity is a communal faith—a team sport. In the final verses of Matthew's Gospel, Jesus tells his disciples to "Go therefore and make disciples of all nations" (Matt. 28:19)—to bring more ministers into the community of faith. When his disciples tried to stop a man who had been casting out demons in Jesus's name, Jesus warned them about dissension among teammates, saying, "Whoever is not against us is for us" (Mark 9:40). Teammates must focus on their common goals, not on those factors that divide them. Following the symbolic birth of the church at Pentecost, the first believers gathered as a community and "had all things in common" (Acts 2:44b). In 1 Corinthians Paul chides the church in Corinth for celebrating the Lord's Supper as a sort of brown-bag lunch in which each person eats what he or she brings instead of sharing his or her provisions with the entire community (1 Cor. 11:17–22.) Ministry is not the job of a select few, nor is ministry done alone. All Christians are ministers, and all ministers must work together to do God's will on earth.

When one is part of a team, one must set aside a desire for individual accolades and achievements and commit to the team's common goal and purpose. One must understand one's role and the value of one's role to the team. Teammates must work together, support one another, and respect one another. This is true in any number of sports, and it is true in the church—the body of Christ.

6

TOUCHING THE ROCK

A People of Ritual and Tradition

You know it's game time when you get on the bus
and go up there and touch that rock.

—CLEMSON UNIVERSITY RUNNING BACK C. J. SPILLER

For I received from the Lord what I also handed on to you,
that the Lord Jesus on the night when he was betrayed took a loaf of
bread, and when he had given thanks, he broke it and said,
"This is my body that is for you. Do this in remembrance of me."
In the same way he took the cup also, after supper, saying,
"This cup is the new covenant in my blood. Do this, as often as you
drink it, in remembrance of me." For as often as you eat this bread and
drink this cup, you proclaim the Lord's death until he comes.

—1 CORINTHIANS 11:23–25

GOING BANANAS

When I was a swimmer at Perry Meridian High School in Indianapolis our team had two premeet rituals. The first was taking a knee and saying the Lord's Prayer. A public high school sports team praying together before competitions may, for some, be an affront to the U.S. Constitution's prohibition of laws "respecting an establishment of religion," but in my homogeneous suburb no one questioned the practice. Several members of the team were not regular churchgoers, but they nonetheless were familiar with the Lord's Prayer and had no issue reciting it before a meet. The ritual was as much about team unity as centering ourselves religiously.

As we said our "amens" and rose to our feet we began the second ritual by clapping in unison a simple rhythm. We continued the rhythm as we emerged from the locker room, and, as we made our way onto the pool deck, we chanted, "Go bananas; go, go bananas." Still clapping and chanting, we gathered in a circle behind the starting blocks. One at a time, senior members of the team would jump into the circle, and each would follow his teammates' charge to "go bananas." It was a childish ritual that we actually ripped off from another team,[1] and I'm sure that our opponents had several laughs at our expense after watching us go bananas. But the ritual was nonetheless an effective way to ease our nerves and build energy before a meet.

Nothing about the prayer or the clapping and chanting had any direct impact on our performance in the pool. No one believed that a brief prayer before a meet would give God cause to intervene on our behalf. Ritual or no ritual, our success in the pool would depend on strength, timing, technique, and months of practice and conditioning. But I would never suggest that our precompetition rituals were not important. Praying and then clapping while our team captains bounced around were integral parts of the Perry Meridian Falcon swimming experience. In an individual sport where swimmers race against the clock and the other people in the pool—both their teammates and the opposition—these rituals reminded us that our performances in our individual events were only important in so far as they contributed to the team's overall score.

TOUCHING THE ROCK

Dr. Greg Carr, a professor at Howard University, told his school's newspaper, *The Hilltop*, in 2003, "Ritual is the established form of ceremony. It's an attempt to order reality."[2] According to Carr, such attempts to order reality apply as much to sports teams as they do to religious communities. "A pre-game ritual is an extension of the game,"

Carr said in the same article. "In a pre-game ritual, you have things you can control. You may not have that control over things in the game."[3] Athletes practice, watch film, and meet to discuss their game plan so that they will have as much control as possible in competition. Teams can run plays dozens of times during practices leading up to the big game, runners and swimmers can rehearse their races, and golfers can walk the course on the eve of a tournament. Players can control whether they run the right routes, box out when a shot goes up, hit the cutoff man, and save some energy for the last hundred meters of the race. But during a competition things happen. Athletes have no control over the weather, an opponents' strengths and weaknesses, decisions made by referees when the correct call is not obvious, nor how team-mates and opponents will react when a play breaks down or a ball takes a funny bounce. Athletic competition is fraught with variables. On the other hand, players and teams have complete control over whether they gather for prayer, touch a plaque on their way out of the tunnel, or end their warm up only after draining a three-pointer.

Rituals and traditions are prevalent throughout sports and are prac-ticed by teams and individual athletes alike. During Michael Jordan's best years with the Chicago Bulls, he ritually wore his practice shorts from his days at the University of North Carolina underneath his uni-form.[4] Former Indiana Pacers star Reggie Miller was known for his elaborate and unusual rituals. Miller adhered to a strict and scripted regimen of warm-up drills and tape-watching sessions during the hours leading up to a game. In a 2005 article for *Sports Illustrated* Chris Ballard described the culmination of Miller's pregame routine:

> Between 30 and 40 seconds before introductions he always goes to midcourt, faces the opponent's basket, dribbles between his legs until the buzzer sounds, then hoists a fadeaway three-pointer. If he misses that, he fires one more three; if he misses that, he shoots a layup.[5]

Reggie would then have the Pacers' media-relations director give him either a Pepsi or a Sprite, depending on the outcome of the previous game, after which point Miller and the media director exchanged play-ful verbal jabs.[6]

Hall-of-fame baseball player Wade Boggs, whose career included long stints with the Boston Red Sox and New York Yankees,[7] religiously ate poultry before every game, earning him the nickname "Chicken Man." Boggs, who was a third baseman for much of his career, took exactly 150 ground balls during infield practice; before every plate appearance, he wrote the Hebrew word *chai* (living) in the dirt with his left foot. Boggs was known to have dozens of other game day rituals that he practiced faithfully throughout his career.[8]

Individual athletes' rituals are often dismissed as superstitions, and "superstition" may be an apt description for many of the more bizarre practices.[9] But team rituals tend to be more substantial. Team rituals unite several persons who are working toward a common goal; they give the team a sense of unity and purpose and remind individual players that they are part of something bigger than themselves. To borrow language from Kenda Creasy Dean and Ron Foster in *The Godbearing Life*, rituals and traditions define a group of people as a communion and not just a community. According to Dean and Foster, "A community's identify depends on common characteristics, interests, and history."[10] In other words a fan club or a school's student body would be a community. A communion is something more. "While communities can exist without intimacy, communions cannot. . . . [In] communions we . . . take on the lives of one another—we participate in a common life . . . and experience the joys and pains of others as though they were our own."[11]

Dean and Foster speak of communion in a purely spiritual sense and name the sacraments of baptism and the Eucharist as rituals that bind people as part of a communion. While no tradition is truly analogous to a Christian sacrament, rituals such as team prayers and pregame dances have the effect of bringing people together in meaningful ways.

The haka—a type of Maori dance—has become a popular pregame ritual for college football teams in the American West and is most commonly associated with Brigham Young University (BYU) and the University of Hawaii. In the case of BYU the idea of doing the haka before games came from wide receiver Bryce Mahuika, grandson of a Maori tribal chief, back in 2005. Mahuika offered the idea in response to coach Bronco Mendenhall's emphasis on team unity. The haka ritual became a means of building communion.[12]

Like my early-nineties Perry Meridian Falcons swim teams, the Immaculata Mighty Macs ritually prayed before each competition. Cathy Rush, who coached the small, Catholic, all-women's college to three national championships (and five title games) in the early 1970s, said in her 2008 Hall of Fame acceptance speech, "Our team, like so many Catholic schools, started with a prayer. And at the end of the prayer there were all—I'm Baptist—all these people to pray for you, which I didn't understand. St. Christopher . . . and the other one was, 'Our Lady of Victory pray for us.' And I joked with my mom, who was also a coach, . . , 'These girls start with a prayer then play like hell.'"[13] The Mighty Macs' pious pregame routine may have seemed incongruous with their physical play on the court, but it centered them and gave them a sense of place and identity.

Football players at Clemson University in South Carolina before each home game rub Howard's Rock and run down the hill that overlooks Memorial Stadium, where the Tigers play. Several decades ago Lonnie McMillan, coach at Presbyterian College (also in South Carolina), nicknamed Memorial Stadium "Death Valley," because it was where his teams went to die. Some years later, as legend has it, a Clemson alum driving through the real Death Valley in California picked up a large, white rock and took it back to Tigers football coach Frank Howard. Howard gave Gene Willimon, executive secretary of Clemson's booster club, the job of disposing of the rock. Willimon instead decided to place it on a pedestal at the top of the hill that led down to the stadium. The day the rock was unveiled, toward the beginning of the 1966 season, Clemson rallied to overcome an eighteen-point deficit in the second half against conference rival Virginia. Soon, touching "Howard's Rock" before each home game became a Clemson ritual. The tradition of running down the hill predates Howard's Rock and arose because the hill was the most direct route from the locker room to the field.[14]

Clemson's pregame traditions may not make sense to outsiders, but they have a profound effect on the players. Running back C. J. Spiller (a junior at the time of this writing) said in a 2007 ESPN.com article, "It's very emotional going up there [on top of the hill]. You know it's game time when you get on the bus and go up there and touch that rock." Former Tigers kicker David Treadwell, in the same article, attributed Clemson's success at Memorial Stadium to the team's pregame ritual. "Clemson's record at home is not a coincidence. Running down the hill is a part of that record."[15]

One of the reasons that this ritual is so meaningful to the players who have participated in it is the fact that it has stood the test of time. Clemson tight end Alex Pearson, a South Carolina native and lifelong Clemson fan, said in an ESPN.com article that he'd dreamed his "whole life" about being able to touch Howard's Rock. "When you rub the rock, you can picture everybody else who's done it in the past doing that."[16] (By contrast, "Go Bananas" lasted only a few years.)

OCTOPI ON THE ICE

Sports rituals aren't limited to the athletes themselves. At Chicago's Wrigley Field the "Bleacher Bums," rowdy Cubs fans who sit in the stadium's outfield bleachers, ritually return every home run ball hit by the opposing team to the field of play. Thus when you watch a Cubs game on WGN (available through most basic cable packages) and you see a visiting player hit the ball over the ivy-covered brick wall, moments later—without fail—you will see it fly right back over the ivy and into the outfield.

Students at Texas A&M University gather on the evening before each home football game for Midnight Yell practice. Students file into Kyle Field (the school's football stadium), and "yell leaders" who have been elected by their peers lead the group in songs and chants. At the close of the festivities, the lights go out in the stadium, and the students in the stands kiss their dates.[17]

Fans of the NHL's Detroit Red Wings ritually throw octopi onto the ice before playoff games (and some regular season games) and after goals are scored. The ritual originated during the 1952 Stanley Cup playoffs. Back then the playoffs consisted of only two best-of-seven rounds. To win the cup, a team had to win eight games. An octopus, of course, has eight legs. Peter Cusimano, who according to legend threw the first octopus (he was a Detroit-area fish monger at the time), said in a 1996 New York Times article, "It was like a good luck omen. The octopus has eight legs, and we were going for eight straight."[18] That year the Red Wings swept both series, winning eight straight. The ritual stuck. My hometown Nashville Predators, one of the Red Wings' division rivals, have borrowed this tradition and modified it, using a catfish instead of an octopus. (I suppose you could call Predators fans "copycatfish." Sorry about that.) Throughout hockey, fans throw hats onto the ice whenever a player scores three goals in a game. The "hat trick" tradition goes back to a hat manufacturer that awarded a hat to any of its home-team players who achieved the elusive goal of scoring three times in a game.

Fans of the 1970s Immaculata teams ritually banged on buckets during Mighty Macs games. Dr. Frank Breen, a fan of the Mighty Macs who traveled with the team during its championship runs, told me that fans of the team, including many of the nuns who worked at the college, needed an effective way to make noise (in addition to the one fan who ritually blew an alpine horn). "[Mighty Macs player] Rene Muth Portland's father owned a hardware store. Rene's parents came to all of Immaculata's games and one day on a lark her father brought a bucket from his store and beat on it with a wooden stick. That started it. Everyone wanted a bucket and so he became the official bucket-and-stick provider, bringing a couple dozen to each game. Could we make a racket, fans and nuns beating and rocking in unison!"

There are several other examples of rituals faithfully practiced by fans and boosters. The Ohio State Marching Band, before or during halftime of every Buckeyes home football game, spells Ohio in script letters with a sousaphone player from the senior class dotting the "i." During the week before every Notre Dame football game, select students paint the players' helmets with a fresh coat of gold-flecked paint. During the middle of the eighth inning of every Boston Red Sox home game, the Fenway Park public address system blasts the Neil Diamond classic "Sweet Caroline" while fans sing along, very few of them relying on the lyrics shown on the scoreboard.

Fans hope that these rituals will inspire their teams and bring them good fortune. But the rituals persist even when the teams disappoint. Fans don't practice these rituals because they produce wins, but because these rituals give fans a sense of place and identify.

MEANS OF GRACE

There is no way to explain rationally how touching a rock, doing a dance, throwing an octopus on the ice, or "going bananas" would affect a team's performance on the field, on the court, or in the pool. Similarly, there is no rational explanation for why celebrating Holy Communion or reciting a creed in unison brings members of a religious community close to one another and to God. Rituals need not make sense to be effective. Trying to understand rationally what happens when one participates in the Eucharist leads to doctrinal and liturgical disputes as well as skepticism and cynicism. The experience of Holy Communion, not the theory, is effective.

Diana Butler Bass, in *Christianity for the Rest of Us*, looks at qualities of thriving mainline Protestant congregations. She found that, in healthy mainline churches, "worship had moved eighteen inches: from the head to the heart."[19] Ritual is most powerful when it is experiential rather than cerebral.

Eastern Orthodox writer Marjorie Corbman explains that ritual is particularly important to today's teenagers and young adults. In *A Tiny Step Away from Deepest Faith*, which she wrote as a teenager, Corbman says, "The distinct feature of my beliefs has always been a mystic leaning, the concept of direct communion with a transcendent and yet omnipresent Reality, whether through meditation or ritual. In fact, this is the distinct feature of the beliefs of most spiritually oriented people of my age."[20]

John Wesley, founder of the Methodist movement in eighteenth century England, referred to rituals and other spiritual practices as "means of grace." Although Wesley believed that God's grace was available to all people at all times, he also felt that God had ordained certain channels through which people could more completely open themselves to God's grace. These means include prayer, baptism, and Holy Communion, among others. Wesley specifically used the word "means" because he wanted to be clear that these rituals were not ends unto themselves. Much as sports rituals do not equal victory on the field, means of grace do not equal salvation. But they are nonetheless important because they are unique ways that we experience God's grace and identify ourselves as God's people. Wesley scholar William J. Abraham explains:

> We might say that means of grace induce us in the knowledge and love of God. . . . They do not atone for sin, nor do they give any ground for merit. We approach them in a spirit of trust, believing that whatever God has promised to give us through them will be delivered to us. What God has promised is grace upon grace.[21]

Christians approach rituals such as communion and reciting creeds with a spirit of trust, not expecting them to have an immediate or tangible effect but knowing that practicing these rituals is simply part of having a relationship with God and being a disciple of Christ. Just as a Clemson football player wouldn't think of not touching Howard's Rock—and just as a Perry Meridian swimmer in the early nineties wouldn't have thought of not clapping while his teammates went bananas—few Christians would consider skipping communion or remaining silent during the Lord's Prayer. In both cases these rituals have become an important part of the community's identity and an important way for members of these communities to connect to something larger than themselves.

"IN REMEMBRANCE OF ME"

Throughout Scripture God and God's people institute rituals that are to be passed down from generation to generation. These rituals are reminders of God's promises to God's people and of the trials and triumphs of their spiritual ancestors. In Genesis, when God established a covenant with Abraham and Sarah and their descendants, God instituted the ritual of circumcision. (See Gen. 17.) The circumcision ritual comes up consistently throughout the Hebrew Scriptures as a means of identifying God's people (or, at least, the men and boys among God's people).[22] Circumcision becomes so synonymous with faithfulness and holiness that, in the New Testament, Paul calls for a metaphorical "circumcision of the heart" (see Rom. 2:29).

The Pentateuch (the first five books of the Christian and Jewish Scriptures) sets out dozens of other rituals that further express the relationship between God and God's people. These rituals involve purification, sacrifice, and reverence. Leviticus explains in great detail the dimensions of altars used for sacrifice and the garments priests are to wear when they intercede with God on the people's behalf. The rituals in the Bible's opening books cover every aspect of ancient Hebrew religious life and clearly demonstrate that the people of Israel are a people set apart—a people fully devoted to God.

Ritual also plays an important role in the story of the early church in the New Testament. In all four Gospels, prior to the beginning of Jesus's formal ministry, we read about John and his ministry of baptism (see Matt. 3:1–12; Mark 1:1–8; Luke 3:1–20; John 1:19–28). Scholars debate the exact purpose of John's baptism and its place in first-century Judaism, but it is clear that pre-Christian baptism somehow involves renewal and repentance. In all four Gospels Jesus begins his ministry by being baptized by John. (See Matt. 3:13–17; Mark 1:9–11; Luke 3:21–22; John 1:29–34.) In the closing verses of Matthew's Gospel Jesus instructs his disciples, "Go forth therefore and make disciples of all nations, baptizing them in the name of the Father and of the Son and of the Holy Spirit" (Matt. 28:19). From very early on baptism has been the church's primary initiation ritual. Acts 2:41 tells of about three thousand converts who were baptized during the traditional birth of the church on Pentecost. In Acts 8 Philip, a newly appointed deacon of the church, baptizes an Ethiopian eunuch who is eager to join the church (Acts 8:26–39).

Holy Communion, which along with baptism is recognized by most Christians as a sacrament (a ritual in which God is uniquely present), also has its roots in the New Testament. During his final meal with his disciples Jesus broke bread, referred to it as his body, and instructed his disciples to eat it. (See, for example, Mark 14:22.) He then passed a cup, referred to the wine as his blood, and instructed his disciples to drink. (See, for example, Mark 14:24.) The earliest reference to the practice of the Lord's Supper or Holy Communion is in Paul's first letter to the church in Corinth, written in the mid 50s:[23]

> For I received from the Lord what I also handed on to you, that the Lord Jesus on the night when he was betrayed took a loaf

of bread, and when he had given thanks, he broke it and said, "This is my body that is for you. Do this in remembrance of me." In the same way he took the cup also, after supper, saying, "This cup is the new covenant in my blood. Do this, as often as you drink it, in remembrance of me." For as often as you eat this bread and drink this cup, you proclaim the Lord's death until he comes. (1 Cor. 11:23–25)

Much as the Clemson football tradition of touching the rock and running down the hill is both a way of remembering the past and preparing for an upcoming game, the Lord's Supper as Paul explains it is both a remembrance of Jesus's sacrifice and a means of actively anticipating Christ's return.

THE SLEEVES STAND FOR HONOR

Because Christianity is a living faith that worships a living God and exists in a constantly changing world, the church's rituals and traditions change over time. Traditions are discarded (the church in which I grew up no longer sings "The Old Rugged Cross" once a month), rituals evolve, and new rituals and traditions take shape. Even the sacraments, which one might describe as the church's most permanent rituals, have changed over time and vary across denominations. (Some churches baptize infants; others only baptize those who are mature enough to profess their faith. Some churches dunk, some sprinkle, and some pour. Some churches celebrate Holy Communion weekly, others monthly, and others less frequently. The breads, wines, and juices used in the sacrament also vary.) Since rituals and traditions are significant in large part because they have staying power, replacing a ritual or altering a tradition can be painful. Just ask any pastor who has been run out of a church for making too many changes to the order of worship. But sometimes these changes are necessary if the church's message is to be relevant across generations and cultures.

Despite Jesus's clear instructions on the subject, I am still unable to forgive my alma mater, the University of Evansville, for what it did to its men's basketball uniforms. In 2002 a new athletic director, Bill McGillis, decided that the Purple Aces would no longer wear sleeves. The Aces had been the only Division I men's basketball team to wear Tshirt-style jerseys. When I was a student there, the crew at Roberts Stadium would play a dramatic monologue about the sleeves over the PA prior to home games. I remember little of what was said about the sleeves, but I do remember, "The sleeves stand for honor, for championships." It was corny for sure, but the sleeves were an important Evansville basketball tradition—a tradition that ended abruptly in 2002.

In defense of McGillis, he eliminated the sleeves in part at the bequest of Aces players. "The day I was hired as athletic director," McGillis said, "I went to the players and asked them about the uniforms. They said to me, 'They gotta go.'"[24] On the other hand (and in my defense), getting rid of the sleeves has done nothing for the team's play on the court. The sleeved Aces earned four bids to the NCAA Tournament and two bids to the National Invitational Tournament (NIT) between 1988 and 1999. The sleeveless Aces have made only one postseason appearance, in the 2009 College Insider Tournament (a tournament for teams not invited to either the NCAA Tourney or NIT). But as soon as a team of Aces players who have been recruited with the promise of not being burdened by fabric on their shoulders makes a run to the Sweet Sixteen, you will be able to count me among those who couldn't care less about the sleeves. Sometimes traditions must change despite the reservations of a few grumpy alumni.

On the other hand, many Christians have found meaning in reclaiming ancient traditions that have been mostly forgotten. I have attended several ministry conferences in recent years where participants have had the opportunity—and have been encouraged—to walk a labyrinth or engage in contemplative prayer. Worship experiences geared toward the postmodern generation often include ancient practices such as burning incense and chanting or singing repetitive choruses. The youth ministry at my church has recovered the tradition of going on pilgrimages. Recently, the youth took a pilgrimage to the Civil Rights Museum in Memphis. The appeal of these ancient rituals may be due in part to the fact that many of them engage the senses in ways that conventional modern worship practices do not, and they give young people different ways to encounter the transcendent. But much of the appeal is also due to the fact that these rituals and traditions are centuries old: They connect the practitioner to a story that spans dozens of generations and continues today.

Sports teams in our postmodern era exhibit a similar need to connect to the past. Consider the number of college and professional teams that pay their respects to history by donning throwback jerseys for big games. My sister was ecstatic when she went to see the Atlanta Hawks play against the Indiana Pacers and found the Hawks wearing the throwback lime-green jerseys from the 1971–72 season. And on more than one occasion during his season with the New York Jets, quarterback Brett Favre attended press conferences wearing a New York Titans cap. (The Jets were known as the Titans during the team's first few seasons in the American Football League.) To commemorate one hundred years as a franchise, hockey's Montreal Canadiens wore every uniform from the team's history during the 2008–09 season. Maybe there is still hope for the Aces' sleeves.

A COMMON LANGUAGE AND A UNIQUE FLAVOR

Rituals and traditions in the church today include the sacraments instituted by Jesus and his earliest followers; common practices such as saying the Lord's Prayer, reciting creeds, and singing a doxology; recovered ancient practices such as contemplative prayer, and going on pilgrimages; and any number of traditions specific to individual congregations. Rituals and traditions frame and structure the worship experience and the life of the church. They provide a common language for Christians across denominations and worship styles, and they give individual congregations a unique flavor. They are borrowed, passed down, retired, rediscovered, and customized.

The same is true of rituals in sports. Quirky pregame habits and fan celebrations make sense to those close to the game. Fans, players, and others involved with sports see nothing unusual about touching a rock or throwing an octopus on the ice because most teams and fan bases have special ways of preparing for competition or celebrating a victory or score. Yet these rituals also have a way of setting apart a team and its fans: You touch a rock, we touch a plaque; you throw octopi, we throw catfish; you do a haka dance, we go bananas.

Anyone who has participated in such rituals and traditions, at church or at the ballpark, understands why they are important, even if their effects are not obvious or tangible. Rituals and traditions are a way of saying, "This is who we are," "This is what we value," and "This is what we hope for." They connect us to the past; give us an identity in the present; and give us a vision for the future.

7

GYM RATS

Perfecting Our Practice

The best advice I can give you is,
"Practice, practice, practice." And when you think you're good
enough, practice some more. And then, when you think
you're as good as you can be, practice some more.

—BASEBALL HALL-OF-FAMER PHIL NIEKRO

Rejoice always, pray without ceasing, give thanks in
all circumstances; for this is the will of God in Christ Jesus for you.
Do not quench the Spirit. Do not despise the words of prophets,
but test everything; hold fast to what is good;
abstain from every form of evil.

—1 THESSALONIANS 5:17–22

PERFECT PRACTICE MAKES PERFECT

"Practice makes perfect" is an old coaching cliché. Legendary football coach Vince Lombardi allegedly added another dimension to this idiom, saying, "Practice doesn't make perfect, perfect practice makes perfect." Lombardi suggests that the quality of one's rehearsal determines the quality of one's performance.

I first came across the Lombardi version of this adage when my sister Whitney brought home a sign bearing the saying that had been created by her seventh-grade basketball coach. The sentiment must have been effective—Whitney's Meridian Middle School Mustangs basketball team went undefeated not only during her seventh-grade year but also during her eighth-grade year. Granted, Whitney's team was led by Katie Douglas, who would go on to win an NCAA title at Purdue and become a WNBA All Star with the Connecticut Sun. Several other players on the team would later play basketball or another sport at the college level. (Whitney, for her part, ran track and cross country at DePauw University, a United Methodist liberal arts school in Greencastle, Indiana.)

Most successful athletes and coaches (and many unsuccessful ones) understand that practice is important and that good practice habits give them the best chance to succeed in competition. Even middle school coaches require players to practice two hours every day after school. High school and college athletic associations dictate the earliest day on which teams can begin practices and the number of hours per week that teams are allowed to practice. Many coaches push these restrictions to the limit, starting practice on the earliest possible date and using the maximum amount of practice time allowed. Most major college basketball programs now hold "Midnight Madness" festivities that begin at 12:00 A.M. on the first day that practice is allowed. These festivities usually involve an informal practice that is open to fans.[1] Premium cable networks such as NBA TV and the NFL Network broadcast preseason practices for fans who want a glimpse of how their favorite teams are shaping up.

NOT DESIGNED FOR YOUR ENJOYMENT

I still have the occasional nightmare about the practice regimen during my four years on the Perry Meridian High School swim team. For much of the season we practiced before school from 5:30 to 6:30 A.M., then after school from 3:30 to 5:00 P.M. We also had two-a-days during Christmas break, practicing from 9:00 to 11:00 in the morning and 3:00 to 5:00 in the afternoon. On the Friday after Thanksgiving we had one three-hour practice in which we wore sweatshirts and tennis shoes—in the pool. Most of our practices consisted of sets of sprints, stroke drills, and long swims to build endurance. On occasion, we would tie bungee cords to the starting blocks and then strap them to our waists and swim toward the other end of the pool against the resistance of the elastic cables, which threatened to jerk us back to the starting wall. Sometimes the coach would have us tread water in the diving well while holding five- or ten-pound weights above our head. Such practice habits undoubtedly improved our performance in the pool. Their effect on our win–loss record is hard to gauge because most of our opponents had similar practice routines.

As a swimmer I looked forward to meets, not necessarily because I craved competition but because meet days meant no practice. I especially looked forward to "tapering" at the end of the season. Tapering is a gradual reduction in yardage and intensity leading up to a big competition. We tapered for about three weeks in preparation for the sectional meet. (As it happened, tapering didn't do me much good; never in my high school career did I qualify for the championship heat in the sectional finals.)

During the first practice scene in the movie *Hoosiers*, Ollie (the smallest and least skilled player on the team, who later ends up the hero of the regional championship) asks Coach Norman Dale during a dribbling drill, "When do we scrimmage?" Coach Dale answers, "We don't scrimmage. And no shooting either." Ollie replies, "That ain't no fun," to which Dale responds, "My practices aren't designed for your enjoyment." Rather, Coach Dale explains, his practices are designed to promote fundamentals and discipline and to condition the players to stay on the court for four quarters without running out of gas. (This is especially important for the Hickory Huskers in *Hoosiers* because the team never has more than seven players.)[2]

Few athletes express a love for practice and conditioning. Toward the end of the 2001–02 NBA season, Allen Iverson, then a player for the Philadelphia 76ers, created one of the most memorable sound bites in recent sports history when he responded to coach Larry Brown's comments about Iverson missing a practice:

> We're sitting here, and I'm supposed to be the franchise player, and we're talking about practice. I mean, listen, we're sitting

here talking about practice, not a game, not a game, not a game, but we're talking about practice. Not the game that I go out there and die for and play every game like it's my last but we're talking about practice man. How silly is that?[3]

(The quote loses a lot of its impact in print. You really need to hear Iverson enunciate the word *practice* to get the full effect of the statement. Clips of the press conference are pretty easy to come by on the Internet. Just search for "Allen Iverson practice.")

Iverson was not dismissing practice entirely, but he clearly did not revere practice as much as did his coach; nor did he feel that his practice habits should be the subject of a press conference. After all, no aspiring young athlete dreams of one day running wind sprints or fielding ground balls hit by an assistant coach. And when players talk about looking forward to the coming season, few are talking about working on their defensive stance in an empty gym or running the same play over and over again on a practice field. Practice is repetitive and often painful, but it is vital to a team or athlete's success.

THE LAST TO LEAVE THE GYM

The bio of almost any all-time great basketball player includes some variation on the line, "[He or she] was always the first player dressed for practice and the last player to leave the gym." The players who are enshrined in the Basketball Hall of Fame in Springfield, Massachusetts, tend to be gym rats. Possibly more than any player in NBA history, Larry Bird was renowned for his practice habits. According to a 1981 *Sports Illustrated* article written just after Bird won his first title with the Boston Celtics:

He begins his routine by setting the ball down by his feet—lovingly, if that is possible—and then jumping rope vigorously for five minutes to warm up. . . . Now he finds himself making layups, 10 with his right hand, 10 with his left. No misses. Then hooks from eight feet, 10 and 10, no misses. He backs away along the right baseline for 15-foot jump shots. . . . He continues to move "around the world" all the way back to the right baseline, making 10 15-footers without a miss . . . . From 20 feet he makes 16 of 20, and then he begins all over again, running up and down, dribbling the ball between and around his legs, heaving it off a wall every now and then, putting it down for the jump rope, then calling it back into action.[4]

Bird's practice regimen obviously paid off. He was three times the NBA's Most Valuable Player, twice the MVP of the NBA Finals, twelve times an All-Star, and three times the winner of the NBA's Three-Point Shootout. His commitment to practice enabled him to hit from anywhere on the court in almost any situation. According to former Celtics coach K. C. Jones, with five seconds left in a tied game against the Seattle Supersonics, Bird found Sonics star Xavier McDaniel following a timeout and said, "Xavier, I'm getting the ball. I'm going to take two dribbles to the left. I'm going to step back behind the three point line and stick it." Sure enough, Bird got the ball, stepped behind the line, and hit the shot over McDaniel.[5]

Considering Christian teachings on pride, I would not suggest you mimic Bird's cockiness in your next church-league basketball game. The point is: If you practice hard enough and well enough, you can be confident that, when you get the ball as the clock runs down in a close game against First Baptist, you will hit the shot. No smack-talking required.

Obviously, the benefits of "perfect practice" are not limited to basketball. During the 2008 Olympics in Beijing, as Michael Phelps was winning eight gold medals and setting seven world records—near perfection in the minds of many—viewers around the world learned about the swimmer's unparalleled practice regimen: a regimen that includes swimming fifty miles per week and not taking days off. Bob Bowman, who has coached Phelps since he was a child, theorized that, by swimming seven days per week, Phelps would be one-seventh more conditioned than his competitors.[6] (I don't know if Bowman ever made Phelps practice in a sweatshirt and tennis shoes.) Phelps' rigorous training routine obviously paid off in the pool. In several events his victory was never in doubt, and he won handily. In other events, such as the 100-meter butterfly, Phelps had to rely on timing and technique to out-touch his opponents, timing and technique that he'd developed during countless hours of training.

In his book *Friday Night Lights* Buzz Bissinger describes the football program at Permian High School in Odessa, Texas, as "perhaps the most successful football dynasty in the country—pro, college, or high school."[7] Between 1965 and 1993 Permian won six state titles and two unofficial national titles, winning over 86 percent of its games along the way.[8] Yet, as Bissinger explains, "All this wasn't accomplished with kids who weighed 250 pounds and were automatic major-college prospects, but with kids who . . . had no special athletic prowess. . . . But they were fearless and relentlessly coached and from the time they were able to walk they had only one certain goal in their lives. . . . Whatever it took, they would play for Permian."[9] A relentless commitment to discipline, fundamentals, and conditioning won state titles. Perfect practice made perfect.

WITHOUT CEASING

Practice might seem out of place in a religion such as Christianity, which believes in salvation by grace rather than works. Paul consistently told his readers that salvation is available only through grace because "all have sinned and fall short of the glory of God" (Rom. 3:23). If we all fall short and are incapable of not falling short, what's the point of practicing? What exactly are we practicing for?

The purpose of practice in sports is to give an athlete every possible (legal) advantage in competition, and therefore the best possible chance of winning. An athlete who practices hard honing skills and conditioning the body can approach competition knowing that her or she has done everything necessary to prepare. Win or lose, that athlete can walk away from that competition without regret, though not necessarily without disappointment. If one approaches competition after skipping workouts and cutting corners, even a victory seems unrewarding.

While Christians don't practice to gain an advantage over competition, they practice because they desire to do everything that is necessary and possible to more fully experience God's grace and to grow in their relationships with God and as disciples of Christ. Paul, in his first letter to the church at Thessalonica (which many scholars believe to be the oldest writing included in the New Testament), closes by encouraging his readers to practice their faith incessantly:

Rejoice always, pray without ceasing, give thanks in all circumstances; for this is the will of God in Christ Jesus for you. Do not quench the Spirit. Do not despise the words of the prophets, but test everything; hold fast to what is good; abstain from every form of evil. (1 Thess. 5:16–22)

Paul's encouragement to "pray without ceasing" has special significance in the Eastern Orthodox Tradition. Many eastern Christians strive to follow this command literally by reciting the Jesus Prayer (or Prayer of the Heart) incessantly until it takes root in their subconscious and saying the prayer becomes as natural as breathing. The prayer has several variations, the most common of which is, "Jesus Christ, son of God, have mercy on me, a sinner." Like many of us in the West, poet and Orthodox layman Scott Cairns owes his familiarity with the Jesus Prayer to J. D. Salinger's 1961 novel *Franny and Zooey*. Cairns, in his book *A Short Trip to the Edge*, describes the prayer as a training exercise: "An established practice of deliberate, overt repetition of the prayer leads to the establishment of an habitual, internal repetition, and that repetition . . . trains the one who so prays to be increasingly aware of God's unfailing presence."[10]

Practicing the Jesus Prayer, much like practicing a zone blocking scheme or a pick-and-roll, is often tedious and sometimes even frustrating. In Salinger's novel, Franny's obsession with internalizing the prayer disrupts her relationships with her boyfriend and family. Cairns, describing his second trip to Mount Athos (a sacred pilgrimage site for Orthodox Christian men), recalls his frustration with the prayer: "After years of saying the prayer, I still hungered for unceasing prayer; I didn't think I had made much progress—except, perhaps, an increasing hunger to know always that sweet sense of God's presence, which I have tasted only fleetingly, intermittently."[11]

Many Orthodox Christians pray this prayer using a chotki or prayer rope—a loop, usually of black wool, of knots or beads that one uses to count the number of times one says the Jesus Prayer. Cairns explains that, while a prayer rope is by no means necessary for practicing the Jesus Prayer, "Focusing on moving your thumb and forefinger from one knot to the next actually assists in focusing the words of the prayer, mostly because this simple activity of the hand helps keep the mind from wandering elsewhere."[12] Most athletes know how one's ability to focus affects the quality of one's practice; most also know the difficulty of staying focused while doing exercises that are rote and repetitive.

Practice, whether athletic or spiritual, is neither easy nor fun; often it is the opposite. (Try swimming for three hours in a sweatshirt.) And even those with the most faithful and disciplined practice habits don't immediately reap the fruits of their labors.

PERFECT [CHRISTIAN] PRACTICE MAKES [CHRISTIAN] PERFECT[ION]

The Jesus Prayer is just one of any number of meaningful Christian spiritual practices. A Christian's practice regimen might include reading and studying the Scriptures, participating in worship, fasting, keeping the sabbath, serving others, and responsible stewardship of money, time, and God's creation. These are the ways in which Christians focus on the fundamentals: love of God and neighbor. These are the ways in which Christians discipline themselves so that they can focus more completely on living lives of discipleship. These are the ways in which Christians work toward perfection.

In the minds of some Christians—and this is where my Wesleyan bias shows—perfect practice makes perfect, not only on the field or the court or the track, but in one's walk with God. John Wesley, the founder of the Methodist movement, preached complete sanctification, the idea that one can defeat evil and achieve true holiness in this lifetime. When Wesley spoke of sanctification he didn't hesitate to use the word "perfection." He believed that perfection was possible. After all, Jesus told his followers to "Be perfect, therefore, as your heavenly Father is perfect" (Matt. 5:48) and encouraged the rich young man to strive for perfection by selling his possessions (19:21). Paul encouraged the Christians in Corinth to perfect their holiness (2 Cor. 7:1) and prayed that they would become perfect (13:9). But Christian perfection for Wesley was a matter of the mind and heart; it didn't involve a complete elimination of sin but a reorientation of one's thoughts, feelings, and attitudes.

Aside from describing "practice," "perfect" enters the sports lexicon as a way to name performances that are as good as the rules of the game allow. One can bowl a perfect game by bowling twelve consecutive strikes and earning a score of 300, the highest score possible. A baseball pitcher can throw a perfect game, facing exactly twenty-seven batters and allowing none of them to reach base. A quarterback in professional football can earn a perfect passer rating—158.3—by completing at least 77.5 percent of his passes, gaining at least 12.5 yards per pass attempt, achieving a touchdown-to-attempt ratio of at least 0.11875, and throwing no interceptions.[13] A basketball player can be perfect from the field, hitting every shot that he or she attempts. A team can complete a perfect season by going through its schedule without any losses or ties.

For the most part these perfect feats are rare, or at least exceptional. And though none of these feats could be accomplished without a devotion to practice, coaches who preach that "perfect practice makes perfect" don't expect their players to pitch a perfect game or earn a 158.3 passer rating every time out. Players strive for performances free from error but understand that, even on their best night, they may give up a few hits or miss the occasional shot. Likewise, even the most devout and disciplined Christians know that, while they aim to live free of sin and keep all of their actions in line with God's will, they cannot be entirely sinless. Wesley understood this. Wesley's notion of Christian perfection was not akin to pitching a perfect game. Rather, it was more like the perfection that players such as Larry Bird achieved on the basketball court. Bird didn't hit every shot, but he hit most of them, and he hit plenty of shots in crucial moments. He took the occasional bad shot and was guilty of the occasional turnover, but his passion and effort and confidence were never in doubt. Bird was the player that his coaches and teammates would look to when the game was on the line. He was perfect, not in his ability to never make a mistake or miss a shot, but in his attitude and approach to the game. The same can be said of any number of players in any number of sports whose perfect practice habits enabled them to be perfect performers on the field, court, or track. Likewise, a perfect Christian is not without sin, but is confident in his or her identity as a child of God and a disciple of Christ, fully devoted to growing in faith through persistent practice.

Through the practice of prayer we bring ourselves before God and receive guidance from our Creator. Through the practices of worship and Holy Communion we unite with Christ as we unite with our brothers and sisters in faith. Through the practice of service, we show our love of God by extending love to our neighbors. Through the practice of hospitality, we emulate Christ by embracing and welcoming God's children. Through the practices of fasting and abstinence, we remember that we are completely dependent on God, and we separate ourselves from those things that distract us from God. But practices such as prayer, worship, and fasting are not in and of themselves effective. We must give ourselves fully to God in prayer; we must be fully present in worship; we must give of ourselves and our gifts with a generous and cheerful heart (2 Cor. 9:7). By perfecting our practice, we perfect our faith. These practices are means by which God sanctifies us and makes us holy.

"PERFECT PRACTICE," NOT PERPETUAL PRACTICE

While American sports culture tends to celebrate athletes who don't take days off, it is important to clarify that "perfect practice" does not mean perpetual practice. Nor does it mean adopting habits that give one an edge but have adverse effects on one's health or well-being. Although I raised up Michael Phelps's rigorous practice regimen earlier in this chapter, as a proponent (if not always a practitioner) of sabbath rest, I have reservations about his insistence on practicing seven days per week. Yet no one would describe Phelps's practice habits as unsafe. The same cannot be said about the many athletes who have hurt, or even killed, themselves by pushing too hard (or being pushed too hard). Football and soccer players during training camps in the intense heat of summer have been known to collapse or die when they are not allowed (by their coach or themselves) sufficient water or rest.

Jockeys and wrestlers must maintain a specific weight and sometimes feel pressure to lose several pounds in a matter of days or hours. Too often these athletes adopt habits such as forced sweating and induced vomiting to drop weight quickly. Laura Hillenbrand, in *Seabiscuit: An American Legend*, describes jockeys in the 1920s and 1930s taking laxatives and even swallowing tape worms to meet weight requirements.[14] While these practices have the short-term benefit of making an athlete eligible for competition, they can have severe negative consequences—both in terms of health and athletic performance—in the long term.

Athletes at all levels risk pushing themselves too hard during the off-season and end up burning out before the end of the season or injuring themselves along the way, especially if they practice without the guidance and supervision of a good strength and conditioning coach. As a high school swimmer, I knew and heard about swimmers who had over-worked themselves and had nothing left when sectionals came around. (Full disclosure: Practicing too hard was never a problem for me.)

Sports obviously is not the only realm in which overexerting one-self is dangerous and burnout is common. Workaholics exist in all professions, and people in all walks of life take extreme measures to get ahead. The Jewish and Christian traditions believe in observing sabbath, setting aside a day or time for rest. The concept of sabbath makes its first appearance in the opening pages of the Jewish and Christian scriptures: "And on the seventh day God finished the work that he had done, and he rested on the seventh day from all the work that he had done. So God blessed the seventh day and hallowed it, because on it God rested from all the work that he had done in creation" (Gen. 2:2–3). "Remember the sabbath day, and keep it holy" (Exod. 20:8) is one of the Ten Commandments, and it extends to servants, livestock, and "the alien resident in your towns" (20:10). The holiness code in the Book of Leviticus mandates a sabbath year in which the land would be given a rest (Lev. 25:1–7). Following the death of John the Baptist, Jesus said to his disciples, "Come away to a deserted place all by your-selves and rest a while" (Mark 6:31). The book of Hebrews says, "A sab-bath rest still remains for the people of God; for those who enter God's rest also cease from their labors as God did from his" (Heb. 4:9–10).

Keeping sabbath is a practice unto itself. One grows closer to God not only by actively doing but also by resting. Sabbath is a means of centering oneself, of reorienting oneself to God. It is also a means of abstaining from activities that might separate a person from God's will for his or her life. Sabbath affirms that one's value does not depend on the quantity of one's work; one's value comes from God.

NEVER MIND ALLEN IVERSON

Regardless of what Allen Iverson tells you, practice is important, both for athletes and for people of faith. Though it can be tedious and painful, practice conditions us and prepares us; it enables us to make the most of our gifts and abilities. Practice is a means by which we go on to perfection, whether bowling a perfect game or experiencing sanctification.

However, practice by itself is not sufficient. The quality of our practice matters. Effective practice requires discipline, commitment, and persistence. After all, in the alleged words of Vince Lombardi, "Practice doesn't make perfect, perfect practice makes perfect."

In athletics practice takes several forms, depending on the sport one plays. It may involve wind sprints, tip drills, batting practice, or a six-mile run. For Christians, practice includes prayer, worship, service, reading and studying the Scriptures, and other acts of mercy, justice, and devotion that we learn from God's people in the Scriptures. Much as athletes grow as runners or swimmers or tennis players through a devotion to quality practice, Christians grow in relationship to God and others through a devotion to practices of the faith.

8

THE DREADED ASTERISK*

Playing the Game with Integrity

Yes, it's legal, but do you really think it's OK?

—PHIL MARTELLI, ST. JOSEPH'S MEN'S BASKETBALL COACH,
on college basketball's ambiguous recruiting rules

"All things are lawful," but not all things are beneficial.
"All things are lawful," but not all things build up.

—1 CORINTHIANS 10:23

THE NOT-SO-VALUABLE ROOKIE CARD

When I was a young baseball-card collector in the late 1980s, some of the hottest cards to own bore the image of Oakland A's star Mark McGwire. In his first season in the majors, McGwire hit a league-leading forty-nine home runs and took home American League Rookie of the Year honors. My goal as a collector was to stock up on the rookie cards of promising young players with the hope that some of these players would go on to hall-of-fame careers and their cards would accordingly increase in value. In my eleven-year-old mind, McGwire was a sure thing. As far as I was concerned, the eventual sale of my 1987 Mark McGwire Topps rookie card would fund my retirement.

During the next decade McGwire went through some ups and downs but by 1998 had regained his place as one of baseball's most talented and interesting players. During the 1997 season McGwire had led the league with fifty-eight home runs, just three short of the hallowed single-season mark set by Roger Maris in 1961. The following season McGwire—and a handful of other players including Sammy Sosa and Ken Griffey Jr.—seemed poised to break the decades-old record. Early in September of that year McGwire, now playing for the St. Louis Cardinals, hit number sixty-one and sixty-two to tie, then break, the record. The Cardinals were playing Sosa's Chicago Cubs when McGwire broke the record, and Sosa memorably ran in from the outfield to congratulate his rival. For his part Sosa hit his sixty-second homer later that month. At season's end, Sosa had sixty-six home runs, five more than the previous record held by Maris, and won the National League MVP award. McGwire had seventy homers, setting a new record that seemed at the time unbreakable.

The record was not unbreakable. Barry Bonds broke it in 2001, hitting seventy-three home runs. In the meantime, McGwire was named as one of the infielders on Major League Baseball's All-Century Team. McGwire, along with Bonds and Sosa, were on track to be first-ballot hall-of-famers and to go down in history as some of the game's all-time greats.

Then steroids happened.

Actually, steroids had been happening, but it wasn't until records were shattered and fifty-home-run seasons became commonplace that people started to ask questions. For years, two of the most hallowed records in all of sports were baseball's single-season home-run record and baseball's all-time home-run record—until recently held by Hank Aaron, who hit 755 in his career. By 2001 the single-season record had been broken twice by significant margins, and several players were quickly climbing the all-time list. McGwire and Sosa each hit more than sixty homers in multiple seasons. Bonds hit seventy-three late in his career after never having hit more than forty-nine in any previous season. Fans and reporters were concerned about the legitimacy of these sacred records and the integrity of the game itself.

During the 2002 season *Sports Illustrated* reported:

Steroid use, which a decade ago was considered a taboo violated by a few renegade sluggers, is now so rampant in baseball that even pitchers and wispy outfielders are juicing up—and talking openly among themselves about it. According to players, trainers and executives interviewed by SI over the last three months, the game has become a pharmacological trade show.[1]

The SI article portrays a sport in which the use of banned substances was commonplace and accepted, in which players didn't even bat an eye when a teammate accidentally spilled a bag containing vials of steroids onto the locker room floor. At the time, Major League Baseball did not test for steroids nor did it have a means of penalizing players who used such substances. The late Ken Caminiti openly and unapologetically admitted to having used steroids during his 1996 National League MVP season with the San Diego Padres.

By 2003 journalists Lance Williams and Mark Fainaru-Wada tagged the nutrition center BALCO as the source of performance-enhancing drugs for many star athletes, including Bonds. In 2006 Williams and Fainaru-Wada published *Game of Shadows*, a book alleging that Bonds had engaged in extensive performance-enhancing drug use. The book actually suggests that Bonds began juicing in response to the praise and publicity that McGwire and Sosa received during the summer of 1998 and the baseball-loving public's obsession with slugging rather than "the complete player who could hit for average and power and who had great speed and an excellent glove."[2] *Game of Shadows* convicted Bonds in the court of public opinion. Many of his peers, including McGwire, suffered the same fate during a 2005 congressional hearing on performance enhancers in baseball. McGwire's famous refusal to "discuss the past" during the hearing was interpreted by many as a confession, as was Sosa's sudden inability to speak fluent English. Rafael Palmeiro, one of the rare players to have three thousand hits and five hundred home runs to his name, vehemently denied using steroids, only to be suspended later that season after testing positive for a banned substance.[3] Jose Canseco, himself an admitted user of steroids and a lightning rod in any discussion of the topic, in 2006 published *Juiced: Wild Times, Rampant 'Roids, Smash Hits, and How Baseball Got*

Big, accusing several high-profile players of steroid use. In 2007 a team led by former Senate Majority Leader George Mitchell released a report naming more than eighty players who may have used performance-enhancing drugs. All-time great pitcher Roger Clemens, who was mentioned several times in the report and in Canseco's book, fought back against doping allegations but, in the minds of many, only made himself appear more guilty. Because of the presumed prevalence of performance-enhancing drug use during a period beginning in the early or mid-1990s and continuing until the middle of the first decade of the twenty-first century, that ten- or fifteen-year span has come to be known as the "Steroid Era."

As the allegations against Bonds, Clemens, and others overshadowed actual play on the field, many baseball fans, writers, and broadcasters looked forward to the day when Yankees star Alex Rodriguez, who is on pace to hit more than eight hundred homers in his career, would shatter Bonds's all-time home-run record and symbolically close the book on the Steroid Era. They presumed that Rodriguez was clean and eagerly anticipated crowning a home run king who had not taken performance-enhancing drugs. Aside from the home run record, Rodriguez was a three-time American League Most Valuable Player and twelve-time All Star who would likely end his career with more than three thousand hits and two thousand RBIs, placing him among the game's all-time greatest players (despite his infamous postseason struggles). But in February 2009 *Sports Illustrated* reported that A-Rod (as Rodriguez is best known) tested positive for steroids in 2003, when Rodriguez was playing for the Texas Rangers. The players who were tested in 2003 were told that the test would be anonymous, that the results would be sealed, and that there would be no punishment for a positive test. But because the test results had been subpoenaed as part of a government investigation, they were not destroyed, and the results of A-Rod's test were eventually leaked. (The names of 103 other players who tested positive are still unknown.) The dream of a clean player holding baseball's most hallowed individual record would have to be put on hold.

Repercussions for illicit activities during the Steroid Era seem mild, given the era's assault on the integrity of the game and its most sacred statistics. As of this writing no players of note have faced long-term

suspensions for steroid use; most of the players who have been suspended under baseball's banned-substances policy have been in the
minor leagues. None of the clean players who lost spots on big-league
rosters to players who cheated have been compensated for lost opportunities. And none of the hallowed home run or strikeout records have
been stricken or amended with an asterisk.

In 1961, when Roger Maris was on pace to hit his sixty-first home
run of the season and break Babe Ruth's record of sixty, then Major
League Baseball commissioner Ford Frick (a big fan of Ruth's) issued
the following statement:

> Any player who may hit more than 60 home runs during his
> club's first 154 games would be recognized as having estab-
> lished a new record. However, if the player does not hit more
> than 60 until after his club has played 154 games, there would
> have to be some distinctive mark in the record books to show
> that Babe Ruth's record was set under a 154-game schedule.[4]

The 1961 season was the first in which American League teams played
162 rather than 154 games. Ruth hit sixty home runs during a 154-
game season; Maris would have an additional eight games to break the
record. In Frick's view the difference in the number of games played
compromised the integrity of the record.

Frick's comments spawned the legend that Maris's record was accompanied in the record books by an asterisk or some other notation.
While no such asterisk ever actually existed—at the time baseball did
not have an "official record book" per se—Frick's statement certainly
called into question the legitimacy of the record. This figurative asterisk has added another layer to the conversation surrounding records set
during the Steroid Era. Simply striking certain statistics from the
record would be problematic because baseball stats are not recorded in
a vacuum. "Going yard" not only adds a home run to a hitter's total and
bolsters his batting average and slugging percentage, it also affects the
pitcher's earned-run average and, in many cases, the win-loss records of
the teams on the field. The same can be said for strikeouts, which have
both a positive effect on the pitcher's stats and a negative one on the
hitter's. Could baseball remove home runs and strikeouts recorded by

players suspected of juicing without also altering the statistics of opposing hitters and pitchers or changing the affected teams' records in the standings? Probably not. But some have argued that baseball could employ an asterisk or other marker that would indicate that certain statistics were recorded during the Steroid Era and therefore their legitimacy has been called into question. (The asterisk itself comes with plenty of problems: If baseball were to mark statistics that had been inflated by steroids, should it also mark statistics that had been deflated by performance enhancers? Consider: "This hitter's on-base percentage would have been higher had he not been facing pitchers who used human growth hormone to get an unfair advantage.")

Alas, baseball's record books contain no asterisks, though many exist in the mental record books of fans and commentators. But the protectors of the game's integrity have found another means, namely Hall of Fame balloting, to punish high profile players who are suspected or guilty of juicing. In 2007, McGwire's first year of eligibility, only 23.5 percent of the members of the Baseball Writers Association of America (the group of writers that elects players to the Hall of Fame) voted for him.[5] In 2008 he improved by a negligible margin, getting 23.6 percent of the vote. Seventy-five percent of voters must vote for a candidate in order for that candidate to be elected. When McGwire retired, many considered him a first-ballot Hall of Famer. But the steroid controversy has clearly changed the minds of many voters, and it is doubtful that McGwire will ever make it to Cooperstown, unless he is eventually selected by the Veterans Committee. (The Veterans Committee, which includes all living members of the Hall of Fame, has the opportunity to elect players who were not elected by the Baseball Writers Association of America.) A similar fate likely awaits players such as Bonds, Sosa, and Clemens.

(As an aside, I personally find it interesting that the concern over banned substances in baseball has been focused almost entirely on individual power-hitting and pitching statistics and not on the outcomes of actual games.)

Baseball is hardly the only sport to have been wrecked by doping scandals (even though it gets most of the steroid-related attention from the American media). Several of the world's best cyclists, including Jan Ullrich, the 1997 Tour de France winner (and five-time runner up) and

2006 winner Floyd Landis, have received lengthy suspensions after testing positive for performance-enhancing drugs. Landis was stripped of his victory. Several track stars have also had victories erased and been hit with suspensions. Perhaps most notably, the International Olympic Committee stripped Marion Jones, winner of a record five track-and-field medals at the 2000 Olympics, of all five medals after she admitted to using performance-enhancing drugs. She had already lied to federal investigators about doping.[6] As of this writing Justin Gatlin, gold-medal winner in the 100 meters at the 2004 Olympics in Athens, is serving a four-year ban from track-and-field.[7] Many suspect that the NFL also has a steroid problem. In 2006 linebacker Shawne Merriman, one of the league's best defensive players, received a four-game suspension for taking an illegal performance-enhancing substance.

LEGAL, BUT NOT OK

The discussion about performance-enhancing drugs in baseball in particular is complicated by a lack of clarity on what was banned when. Some players were no doubt able to gain a seemingly unfair advantage without technically breaking the rules. And baseball is by no means the only sport in which it is sometimes unclear whether a rule has been broken or simply bent.

Recruiting rules in college sports are especially flexible. Many of the best recruiters have become masters of loopholes and gray areas, pushing the rules to their limits and pushing the limits of the rules. While buying gifts for a player is illegal, hiring a player's high school or travel league coach as an assistant is not. Nor is paying a player's father or guardian large sums for speaking engagements or helping at a basketball or football camp. What is legal in college recruiting sometimes falls outside the bounds of what is ethical.[8]

In sports such as basketball and football, where so much is at stake financially for colleges and universities, a coach's job security depends heavily on his or her ability to recruit top players. Hiring a player's father as an assistant coach and paying him thousands of dollars to speak at camps may seem shady, but if a player is good enough, shadiness could mean the difference between a coach getting a contract extension and a coach losing his or her job.

In a 2008 article ESPN.com's Dana O'Neil took a close look at shady recruiting, particularly in college basketball. She discovered that many basketball coaches believe that the solution lies not in more regulations but in peer accountability. St. Joseph University coach Phil Martelli (who is also the husband of former Immaculata College basketball star Judy Marra Martelli) said, "I honestly believe there is a groundswell of people who are willing to pick up the phone and say, 'Yes it's legal, but do you really think it's OK?'"[9]

When rules are unclear or flexible, deciding how far to push them is a matter of integrity. Although St. Paul felt strongly that Christians were free from the restraints of Jewish law, he told the church in Corinth, "'All things are lawful,' but not all things are beneficial. 'All things are lawful,' but not all things build up" (1 Cor. 10:23). Eating meat that had been sacrificed to idols, to borrow an example from Paul's day, was lawful, but it was a source of division in the church and did nothing to bring early Christians closer to God. (See 1 Cor. 8:8–13). Hiring a player's summer-league coach as an assistant may be legal and may help to land a star recruit. But it deviates from the spirit of college athletics that says that a student-athlete should select a school based on all that it has to offer academically and athletically, and that the coaching staff should be the persons most qualified and equipped to teach players and help them grow. Supplements and drugs that have not yet been formally banned by a professional sports team may nonetheless give a player an unnatural and unfair advantage over his or her competition. Not everything that is legal is OK.

CALLING OUR OWN LINES

Integrity in sports is further complicated by the role of the officiating crew. During the course of a competition the team of officials must make several quick decisions to enforce the rules of the game. No matter how skilled or experienced an official may be, no referee is capable of seeing everything that happens on the court or field at one time. An official may not always know with certainty whether the ball grazed the sideline or whether the player touched the ground with at least one foot before falling out of bounds. And in sports that lack the benefit of instant replay, knowing for sure may be impossible.

Whatever the circumstances, an official must, to the best of his or her ability, render a judgment.

In football, when a receiver dives to the ground to make a catch, the catch is only valid if the receiver's hands or arms are underneath the ball. He can use his arms to trap the ball against his body, but he cannot trap the ball against the ground. But whether a player caught the ball or trapped the ball is not always apparent to the official's naked eye. Inevitably an official will sometimes give a player credit for a catch when the player has merely trapped the ball against the ground. Should the player admit to the official that he didn't actually catch the ball? Similarly, basketball players sometimes get away with pushing off or traveling or spending too much time in the lane. Should these players confess their "sins" before the referee?

According to the vast majority of coaches and players (and probably officials), the answer in all cases would be, "No." The burden of making the call falls entirely on the official and a player has no obligation to admit that he or she has gotten away with an illegal play. Integrity, in these cases, would disrupt the flow of the game and damage the credibility of the official in the eyes of the players and fans.

In October 1990 the University of Colorado Buffaloes and University of Missouri Tigers met in a football game that would have conference and national championship implications. Late in the fourth quarter, Colorado drove down the field, trailing 31–27. Only a touchdown could help them. In the game's final minute, Colorado got a first down just short of the goal line. Buffaloes quarterback Charles S. Johnson spiked the ball on first down to stop the clock. Missouri stuffed Colorado running back Eric Bieniemy on second down. But the officials neglected to flip the down marker to indicate third down. So the Buffaloes ran another second down play. Again, Missouri stopped Bieniemy short of the goal line. On third down (which should have been fourth down) Johnson again spiked the ball. Then on fourth down (actually fifth down), the Buffaloes pounded the ball into the end zone, scoring the winning touchdown. The game has since become known as the "Fifth Down Game." Colorado would go on to win a share of the national championship that season, though the memory of that championship has been tainted by the Fifth Down Game. The question is,

What could or should Colorado have done? If they had noticed the error during the game, should they have alerted the officials? Possibly. If they did not learn of the problem until afterward, should they have forfeited the game? Perhaps, but such action would have been unprecedented. Again, the burden falls on the official. If nothing else, then Colorado coach Bill McCartney said eight years after the fact that he was "remorseful" about the outcome of the game.[10]

Not all sports rely so heavily on officials to maintain the integrity of the game. At many levels of play, tennis players are expected to "call their own lines," determining for themselves whether a ball is in bounds or out of play. In such cases, the outcome of a match depends significantly on the integrity of the players. Golfers are responsible for marking their balls so that they will know where to place the ball before taking their next shot. Again, the player's honesty has an impact on the results of the competition.

During a 2008 PGA Tour qualifying tournament, golfer J. P. Hayes noticed that he had used a ball in competition that had not been approved by the United States Golf Association. As soon as he noticed the problem, he reported himself and was disqualified. Prior to the disqualification, Hayes was in good shape to qualify for the PGA Tour. And no one would have had any way of knowing that he had used an illegal ball. His integrity cost him a shot at playing in his sport's most prestigious professional league. Hayes took complete responsibility and also refused to blame his caddie, who had tossed him the illegal ball.[11]

This sort of self-sacrificing honesty would not have a place in every sport. In many team sports or faster-paced individual sports such as tennis, confessing that one has inadvertently gained an unfair advantage is more a disruption than an honorable gesture. A basketball referee would have little patience with players who confessed to walking violations that were not called. A football official likely would not even listen to a wide receiver who insisted that he trapped the ball against the ground instead of catching it cleanly. And if a tennis player were to stop playing to argue that her serve actually landed out of bounds, her opponent could capitalize on the distraction and score an easy point. Many of these sports have a mechanism by which an opposing player or coach or an uncertain official can challenge a questionable call that favored a player or team. That said, J. P. Hayes's confession is still an extraordinary display of integrity and sportsmanship.

God expects us to follow the example of J. P. Hayes—to be people who hold ourselves to a high standard of integrity. God doesn't place the burden on the officials. In Jeremiah God vows to make a new covenant with Israel: "I will put my law within them, and I will write it on their hearts. . . . No longer shall they teach one another, or say to each other, 'Know the Lord,' for they shall all know me" (Jer. 31:33b–34a). Under this new covenant the law is no longer a set of rules but is instead an attitude and way of life. We see this new covenant thinking in Jesus's Sermon on the Mount. He tells his audience, "You have heard that it was said to those of ancient times, 'You shall not murder.' . . . But I say to you that if you are angry with a brother or sister, you will be liable to judgment" (Matt. 5:21a, 22a). Likewise, "You have heard that it was said, 'You shall not commit adultery.' But I say to you that everyone who looks at a woman with lust has already committed adultery with her in his heart" (5:27–28). Jesus is not merely concerned with the law but with the spirit of the law. Instead of merely avoiding sins such as murder and adultery, we need to eliminate the mentality that could tempt us to murder or commit adultery. Instead of merely avoiding banned drugs and substances, one needs to eliminate the mentality to seek an unfair or unnatural advantage, regardless of whether such an advantage is legal.

God is aware of our actions and the spirit in which we act, and God holds us accountable for our indiscretions. This does not mean that we should live life as though the mighty referee in the sky is eyeing us, ready to blow the whistle, but it does mean that we should be honest about the mistakes we make. God offers us grace and forgiveness and is eager to help us turn away from sin but asks that we confess our sins before God and before those we have sinned against and that we seek reconciliation. (See, for instance, Lev. 5:5 and 2 Cor. 5:18–19.)

FACING THE MUSIC

While I have been writing this book, my Tennessee Titans have been putting together what may end up being the best season in franchise history. For much of this run Kerry Collins, a thirty-five-year-old veteran who began the season as a backup, has played quarterback. Although Collins has had a respectable career statistically, he has had several problems on the field (such as throwing four interceptions against the Ravens in Super Bowl XXXV) and off (such as his public struggles with alcoholism) since entering the NFL in the mid 1990s. In a December 2008 column, sportswriter Rick Reilly commends Collins for always having been honest about his mistakes and willing to accept the blame and/or consequences. Reilly writes, "No matter how he screws up his life—and the young Collins found more ways than MapQuest—he always faces the music." By contrast, Reilly goes through a litany of other athletes, including Bonds and Jones, who have made excuses for their wrongdoing.[12]

We would do well to remember that history has judged harshly those athletes who have sought an unfair advantage and have been dishonest about doing so. We should instead strive to be people of integrity who obey the spirit of God's law, not seeking ways to bend or stretch the rules; who face the music without making excuses; and who hold ourselves accountable to God's standard of living.

9

FOR SUCH A TIME AS THIS

Answering the Call

I wasn't standing where I should have been. . . .

So, I could see the ball was going to fall short,

and no one else could.

—NC STATE'S LORENZO CHARLES

on his game-winning dunk in the 1983 NCAA title game

Perhaps you have come to royal dignity

for just such a time as this.

—ESTHER 4:14B

ESTHER IN BASKETBALL SHORTS

Lorenzo Charles was in the right place at the right time. During the final seconds of the 1983 NCAA championship game, with the score tied at 52, Charles was standing under the basket as his North Carolina State Wolfpack teammate Dereck Whittenberg launched a desperation shot from thirty feet out. Actually, by his own admission, Charles was standing in the wrong place. "I wasn't standing where I should have been," Charles told ESPN Classic in a 2003 interview. "I was standing up under the basket, which, as an offensive rebounder, you shouldn't. . . .

So, I could see the ball was going to fall short, and no one else could."[1] Whittenberg's shot fell short—way short, missing the basket entirely. Charles was in the perfect position to retrieve the airball and dunk it. The dunk put NC State ahead of the heavily favored Houston Cougars as time expired and completed one of the biggest championship game upsets in NCAA Tournament history.[2]

Lorenzo Charles's moment of glory was the serendipitous result of his standing in the wrong place and his teammate taking a poor shot. On the evening of April 4, 1983, two wrongs did make a right (so to speak). Charles was in the perfect position to make something happen, and he took advantage of the opportunity. The 6′7″ forward was Esther in basketball shorts. Perhaps he was under the basket "for just such a time as this."

"For just such a time as this" is maybe the best known phrase from the Book of Esther, a book whose title character was a Jew living in the Persian diaspora after the fall of the Babylonian Empire during the reign of King Ahasuerus.[3] The Book of Esther opens with a pair of week-long banquets: one for the men hosted by the king and one for the women hosted by the king's wife, Queen Vashti.[4] On the seventh day of raucous merrymaking, a drunk King Ahasuerus decides he'd like to parade his beautiful wife in front of his banquet guests "wearing the royal crown" (Esth. 1:11). Some rabbinic sources suggest that the king wanted Vashti to appear in front of the crowd wearing only the royal crown. At any rate King Ahasuerus wants to exploit his wife; and Vashti, a feminist more than two millennia before feminism, refuses. Of course, in ancient Persia a woman's refusal to wear the royal crown meant forfeiture of said crown, and Ahasuerus begins his search for a new queen. The search involves bringing in "beautiful young virgins" (Esth. 2:2) and seeing which one "pleases" the king (2:4). "Pleases the king" implies a sexual audition of sorts that would certainly be pleasing to the king but much less satisfying for the young women brought into the royal harem. Esther, the Jew, wins this contest, although her new husband is not aware that she is Jewish.

While Esther settles into the palace in Susa, a fierce rivalry erupts between Esther's relative and father figure Mordecai and Haman, the story's villain and a prominent member of the king's court. Haman's hatred of Mordecai, which intensifies when Haman learns of Mordecai's Jewish faith and heritage, causes him to plot against the Jewish community in Susa (Esth. 3:1–6). Haman convinces the king to issue a decree calling for the destruction of the Jewish people; the king does not realize that both Esther and Mordecai, who has saved the king's life, are Jews. Mordecai understands that Esther, as queen, is in a unique position to bargain with King Ahasuerus to save her people. According to the text, entering the king's inner court uninvited—even if one is the king's wife—is punishable by death. But the queen would be more likely to survive demanding an audience with the king. This realization prompts Mordecai to say to Esther, "Perhaps you have come to royal dignity for just such a time as this" (Esth. 4:14b). Esther, of course, comes through, and her people are victorious.

Because he mistakenly stood directly beneath the basket, Lorenzo Charles was uniquely positioned to retrieve Dereck Whittenberg's airball and score the winning basket. Because Esther was the one who most pleased King Ahasuerus and became royalty against her will, she was uniquely positioned to be an advocate for the Jewish people. While preventing genocide and winning an NCAA basketball championship are hardly comparable, both Esther and Charles discovered in an otherwise unfortunate situation an opportunity to do good.

Most people of faith have learned that devoting oneself to God does not inoculate one against trials and suffering, nor does it prevent one from making mistakes. We all are flawed individuals in a broken world. Being faithful does not mean avoiding adversity but knowing how to respond amid adversity. It also means being prepared to act when our time comes.

OUT OF THE GROCERY STORE AND INTO THE SUPER BOWL

For much of his college career at Northern Iowa, Kurt Warner was the team's third-string quarterback. Warner was finally named a starter his senior year, and in 1993 he had a breakout season in which he was named conference player of the year. Yet he played in Division I-AA (now Division I-FCS[5]) and was largely off the radar of NFL scouts. In 1995 Warner signed with the Iowa Barnstormers of the Arena Football League. The indoor game's fast-paced, high-scoring style allowed

Warner to showcase his passing abilities. After a short but impressive Arena League career, the NFL's St. Louis Rams picked up Warner and sent him to the Amsterdam Admirals of NFL Europe. After one season in Amsterdam, Warner earned a spot on the Rams' roster as a backup quarterback. As he worked his way through football obscurity, Warner bagged groceries at a Hy-Vee grocery store in Cedar Rapids, Iowa, to earn extra money.[6]

Warner, like many backup quarterbacks, was an unknown quantity. He had been an undrafted free agent who'd worked his way into the NFL by playing in football's minor leagues. Warner's job was to stand on the sideline, holding the clipboard, while starter Trent Green took the snaps on the field. Green was coming off of a breakout season with the Washington Redskins. The Rams had signed Green to a big contract, hoping that he'd become a franchise quarterback. Rams fans, if they even knew the name of their team's backup quarterback, would have been content if Warner never left the sideline.

Any hopes that Rams fans had for the 1999 season were put on hold during the preseason when Green went down with a season-ending knee injury. The unknown backup from Northern Iowa and the Arena League would be running the Rams offense, an offense that featured running back Marshall Faulk, a future hall-of-famer who had been recently acquired from the Indianapolis Colts, and talented receivers Isaac Bruce and rookie Torry Holt. On the surface, the Rams' situation looked bleak. The team had put together a lot of young talent (especially on offense), had hired a seasoned head coach in Dick Vermeil, and had put themselves in position to make the playoffs for the first time in a decade; but they'd counted on having Trent Green, not an untested backup, to get the ball to Faulk and the receiving corps. Without Green, few experts expected the Rams to contend for a playoff spot.[7]

Because of a variety of circumstances, some of which were beyond his control, Warner had an opportunity to be a starting quarterback in the NFL. He just had to perform. If he could lead the Rams to a winning season, no one would think less of him for the time he spent in Division I-AA, the Arena League, or the Hy-Vee grocery store.

Warner made the most of the opportunity to be a starter in the NFL. He led the Rams to a 13–3 record, won the league's Most Valuable

Player award, and, most importantly, was the MVP of the Super Bowl, leading the Rams to a 23–16 victory over my Titans, who famously fell one yard short of sending the game to overtime. During the trophy presentation Warner thanked Jesus for the victory, which annoyed me since it implied that Jesus favored the Rams over the Titans, but bothered few others because Warner's story was so incredible. To some, divine intervention seemed the most plausible explanation for Warner's unlikely journey from an Iowa grocery store to Super Bowl MVP.

I would not go as far as to suggest the Kurt Warner is somehow "God's quarterback." (That would involve an assessment of God's role in the injuries that plagued Warner for the better part of a decade following the Rams' Super Bowl victory.) Warner simply had prepared himself physically and mentally (and likely spiritually) to be an NFL quarterback whenever the opportunity arose. And when Warner got the call to take over the starting job for the Rams, he was ready.

A BALLPLAYER WITH GUTS ENOUGH NOT TO FIGHT BACK

Great baseball executive Branch Rickey, a general manager for the St. Louis Cardinals, Brooklyn Dodgers, and Pittsburgh Pirates, had long believed that Major League Baseball, which had been segregated for much of its history, should be integrated. In the mid-1940s Rickey decided the time was right to make it happen. Under the guise of creating a new Negro league, Rickey underwent an extensive search to find the right African American or dark-skinned Latino player to break baseball's color barrier. Eventually Rickey settled on Jackie Robinson.

Robinson had lettered in four sports—baseball, basketball, football, and track—at UCLA and had served stateside in the Army during World War II before playing for the Kansas City Monarchs in the Negro leagues. He had handled himself honorably in standing up to racism and discrimination in the military, even though doing so nearly got him a court-martial. Rickey's choice of Robinson had as much to do with the young player's courage and resolve as it did his prowess on the baseball diamond (see more detail about Robinson in chapter 3). Robinson, in his autobiography, recalls his meeting with Rickey:

> Branch Rickey had to make absolutely sure that I knew what I would face. Beanballs would be thrown at me. I would be called

the kind of names which would hurt and infuriate any man. I would be physically attacked. Could I take all of this and control my temper, remain steadfastly loyal to our ultimate aim?[8]

Robinson asked Rickey, "Are you looking for a Negro who is afraid to fight back?" Rickey boldly replied, "Robinson, I'm looking for a ballplayer with guts enough not to fight back."[9]

Robinson had not expected the color barrier to fall during his lifetime, and he certainly had not expected that he would play the central role in tearing it down. There were bigger stars in the Negro leagues, players like Satchel Paige and Josh Gibson, who would have been more obvious choices to be Major League Baseball's first African American player. But Rickey saw something special in Robinson and felt strongly that he was the right player for the job.

Without even knowing it, Jackie Robinson had spent much of his life preparing himself—both athletically and in terms of his character—to be a leader in the most important movement in sports history: the movement toward integration. By virtue of being the first African American player in the majors, he would receive an extra helping of taunts and threats. But because he had the strength and courage to press on amid hatred and prejudice, he would be able to clear a path on which others could follow.

Robinson found himself in Branch Rickey's office "for just such a time as this." He seized the opportunity to play for the Dodgers, handling himself with dignity and class and impressing baseball fans with his skills as a hitter, fielder, and base runner. Within a couple decades baseball was fully integrated, and Robinson has inspired people of all races across several generations because of his courage, his character, and his skills as a ballplayer.

WHEN GOD COMES CALLING

Scripture gives several examples of persons who, like Esther (and Kurt Warner and Jackie Robinson), found themselves in situations "for just such a time as this"—people who were ready to answer God's call upon receiving that call. Joseph (the one in the Book of Genesis, not the one who raised Jesus) is best known for his coat of many colors. A more accurate translation might be a "long-sleeved robe" or a "striped coat," but the style of the garment is incidental: The coat was a symbol of Jacob's unique love for his eleventh son. "[Jacob] loved Joseph more than any other of his children" (Gen. 37:3a). Because he was his father's favorite, and because he dreamed that he would one day reign over his older brothers (Gen. 37:5–8), his brothers resented him.

Joseph's brothers saw an opportunity to kill him and were tempted to do so before Reuben, the eldest of the bunch, intervened and suggested that they throw their brother in a pit instead. Another of Joseph's brothers, Judah, then decided that leaving Joseph in a pit would be pointless when they could profit by selling him to Midianite traders. So they sold Joseph into slavery and led their father Jacob to believe that his favorite son had been devoured by wild animals. The Midianites in turn sold Joseph to Potiphar, an official working for the Egyptian Pharaoh. Joseph quickly earned Potiphar's favor and was put in charge of his master's household. Eventually, and according to the text because of Joseph's being "handsome and good-looking" (Gene 39:6b), Potiphar's wife attempted to seduce him. When Joseph resisted her advances, she framed him for rape, and Joseph ended up in prison.

In prison Joseph met Pharaoh's chief cupbearer and baker, both of whom had been punished for offending Pharaoh, and both of whom had troubling dreams. Joseph interpreted the dreams, telling the cupbearer that he would be restored to his office and the baker that he would be executed. Both interpretations proved true. Two years later, while Joseph was still in prison, Pharaoh revealed to his cupbearer a dream he'd had about seven thin and seven fat cows. The cupbearer recalled the prisoner who could accurately interpret dreams, and Pharaoh sent for Joseph. Joseph correctly surmised that the seven fat cows represented seven years of plenty in Egypt and that the seven thin cows represented seven years of famine that would follow. Pharaoh trusted Joseph's assessment and appointed the prisoner to oversee Egyptian land use and food supply. Joseph successfully managed the crisis, setting aside food reserves during the years of plenty so that Egypt would be able to survive the years of famine.

When the famine finally arrived, Joseph had risen to a position of significant power. The famine reached Joseph's brothers and fathers in Canaan; so did word that there was food in Egypt. This unfortunate food shortage that Joseph had prepared for so effectively gave him an opportunity to forgive his brothers and save his family. Speaking to his repentant brothers, who had come to Egypt seeking food, Joseph said, "Even though you intended to do harm to me, God intended it for good, in order to preserve a numerous people" (Gen. 50:20). Joseph had experienced misfortune that even a Cubs fan might not manage to endure. His brothers had abused him and sold him into slavery; his master's wife had falsely (but successfully) accused him of rape. But Joseph still made himself available to God, and when his time came Joseph was ready to answer God's call, allowing God to work through him to save his family and guide the entire nation of Egypt through seven years of famine.

Samuel was the son of Hannah, who had waited expectantly for God to bless her with a child. When Samuel was born, Hannah consecrated him and sent him to live with the priest Eli, who would prepare Samuel for a life of service to God. When Samuel was a boy, God called out to Samuel in an audible voice that must have been similar to Eli's. After some confusion, Eli told Samuel that the voice belonged to God, after which point Samuel responded to the voice saying, "Speak, for your servant is listening" (1 Sam. 3:10b). This response, following a childhood of training and preparation, was the beginning of Samuel's career as one of Israel's greatest prophets.

The prophet Isaiah experienced God more clearly than did Samuel. Instead of hearing a nondistinct voice, Isaiah saw a vision of God sitting on a throne surrounded by seraphs. After a seraph cleansed Isaiah's lips with a burning hot coal from the altar, God asked, "Whom shall I send, and who will go for us?" Isaiah responded, "Here am I; send me!" (Isaiah 6:8). When he heard God's call, Isaiah was ready to respond.

The angel Gabriel assigned Mary, a young unmarried girl at the time, the unthinkable task of giving birth to God's own son. Carrying a child out of wedlock was scandalous, and raising God's anointed Messiah was a tall order for anyone. While no one could have been prepared to be the mother of the Christ, Mary was prepared to answer God's call. "Here am I, the servant of the Lord," Mary said to Gabriel, "letay it be twith me according to your word" (Luke 2:38). Mary was ready when God called her number.

Lest we give Esther, Joseph, Samuel, Isaiah, or Mary too much credit for being prepared to answer God's call, none of these biblical heroes would have been ready to respond apart from God's grace. God had been working in the lives of these people long before putting them in a position "for just such a time as this." God worked through their families and mentors (Mordecai for Esther, Hannah and Eli for Samuel, Elizabeth for Mary, and so on) and their life experiences (Joseph had several opportunities to hone his gift of dream interpretation and Samuel grew up under the tutelage of a priest) to prepare them for the day when they would be called to act. God "coached them up," so to speak, much as a coach offers guidance and instruction to an athlete long before asking that athlete to perform in a game. John Wesley would call this preseason coaching "prevenient grace." God is at work in one's life even before one has an awareness of God. We just have to claim the work that God is doing. To use a sports metaphor, we need to buy in to God's system. Like athletes, Christians must follow our coach's practice regimen. This involves spiritual practices such as prayer, worship, and service, which are discussed in more detail in chapter 6.

GOD GIVES US ANOTHER CHANCE TO TAKE THE BIG SHOT

On the other hand, the Scriptures gives several examples of persons—including some of the Bible's greatest heroes—who were not prepared "for just such a time as this." When the Israelites in the wilderness learned that the current occupants of the promised land were giants who lived in heavily fortified cities (Num. 13:26–33), instead of claiming the land that God had promised them, they rebelled against Moses and God and cried out, "Would that we had died in the land of Egypt! Or would that we had died in this wilderness! Why is the LORD bringing us into this land to fall by the sword?" (Num. 14:2b–3a). Because of their reluctance to act when the opportunity arose, the Israelites had to wait a generation before finally entering the promised land. In Caesarea Philippi Jesus gave Simon the name Peter, "The Rock," and said, "On this rock I will build my church" (Matt. 16:18). Peter later told Jesus, "Even though I must die with you, I will not deny you" (Matt. 26:35). Yet, while Jesus was on trial for his life and people recognized Peter as a friend of "Jesus the Galilean," Peter denied his Lord and teacher three times (Matt.

26:69–75, cf. Mark 14:66–72; Luke 22:55–62; John 18:25–27). Even biblical heroes such as Abraham, Sarah, and David had lapses in faith, taking matters into their own hands instead of waiting for God to act in God's good time. (See, for example, Gen. 16:1–6 and 2 Sam. 24:1–17.)

Many athletes wait years for a chance to start or earn a spot on the team only to squander that chance when it arrives. Some—such as playground basketball legend Earl "The Goat" Manigault[10] and talented University of Nebraska running back Lawrence Phillips[11]—were unable to overcome disciplinary issues that had haunted them in the past. Others, for any number of reasons, simply were unable to perform at a high enough level when an opportunity presented itself.

That said, one should not get the impression that people, whether in sports or in life, get just one shot, that one's career or relationship with God depends on how one responds in a singular situation. Larry Bird dropped out of Indiana University, overwhelmed by the size of the campus and put off by a cold reception from older players. After spending more than a year away from college, living in his hometown of French Lick, Indiana, Bird got a second chance at Indiana State University and led the previously unknown and unheralded Sycamores to the NCAA finals. Josh Hamilton came out of high school in 1999 as the number one pick in the Major League Baseball draft, taken by the Tampa Bay Devil Rays. Yet drug addiction kept Hamilton from making the Devil Rays' roster. After a few years in the minor leagues, during which he failed at least four drug tests, Hamilton was out of baseball altogether in 2004. Hamilton successfully completed rehab and fought his way back into the minor leagues toward the end of the 2006 season. That year the Cubs took a chance on Hamilton by acquiring him in the Rule 5 Draft; the Cubs promptly sold Hamilton's rights to the Cincinnati Reds. By rule, players acquired through the Rule 5 Draft had to spend an entire year on their team's major league roster. Hamilton was able to take advantage of the situation, battling through injuries to put together a very respectable rookie season. The Reds traded Hamilton to the Texas Rangers, and in 2008 he was selected as one of the starting outfielders for the American League All-Star Team.[12]

Biblical heroes such as the people of Israel, Simon Peter, Abraham and Sarah, and David, much like Larry Bird and Josh Hamilton, were able to work through their past mistakes and take advantage of new opportunities that came along. God continued to work in and through these people. The Israelites eventually made it to the promised land and established for God a center of worship. Peter became an important leader in the early church and played a key role in the mission to the Gentiles. Abraham and Sarah, despite doubting that God's promise of a son would come true and taking matters into their own hands, proved their allegiance to God and became the grandparents of God's chosen people. David, though he made several lapses in faith throughout his reign, became the greatest king of Israel and would be known as a man after God's own heart (see Acts 13:22). God's grace is persistent, and God does not give up on people. God will give us another chance to make the team or take the big shot.

Still, there is value in preparing one's heart, mind, and body so that one is ready when he or she receives a call to action, whether a call to come off the bench or to do God's work. Jesus told a parable of ten bridesmaids, five wise and five foolish, who were waiting late at night for the bridegroom (Matt. 25:1–13). The five wise bridesmaids came prepared with oil for their lamps, while the foolish bridesmaids had none. When the bridegroom arrived at midnight the wise bridesmaids were able to light their lamps and go out to join him for his banquet. The foolish bridesmaids, by contrast, had to leave to buy oil. By the time they had returned, it was too late, and they were shut out of the bridegroom's banquet.

No one wants to be shut out of the banquet. Athletes don't want to squander an opportunity to make the team or come off the bench and make an important contribution in a big game. Similarly, Christians do not want to pass up an opportunity to grow closer to God or to participate in God's redemptive work on earth. God will continue working in our lives even if we fail to answer God's call, but if we aren't prepared when God comes calling, we'll miss out on all the great things God has in store for us in the meantime.

FOR SUCH A TIME AS THIS

Lorenzo Charles, Kurt Warner, and Jackie Robinson, along with Esther, Joseph, Samuel, and Mary, teach us an important lesson: Be prepared.

You never know when the coach will call your number, when the ball will fall into your hands, when the bridegroom will arrive, or when God will ask you to risk your life to save an entire nation. God is already preparing us for the work that God has in store for us; we just need to be alert so that we'll be ready when God calls us off the bench "for just such a time as this."

10

"DO YOU BELIEVE IN MIRACLES?"

Signs, Wonders, and Transcendent Moments

Do you believe in miracles? Yes!

—ABC BROADCASTER AL MICHAELS
during the final seconds of the United States hockey team's
victory over the Soviet Union in the 1980 Winter Olympics

Jesus looked at them and said,
"For mortals it is impossible, but not for God;
for God all things are possible."

—MARK 10:27

THE PLAY

"The band is on the field!"

To many sports fans those six words evoke images of a chaotic kick return at California Memorial Stadium in the fall of 1982—a kick return known to history as "The Play." The Play was the culmination of 1982's Big Game, the annual football game between Bay Area rivals California (Berkeley) and Stanford. After a Mark Harmon field goal, Stanford, led by future NFL hall-of-famer John Elway, took a 20–19 lead with four seconds remaining. A win would send the Cardinal to Elway's first and only bowl game.

Due to a fifteen-yard penalty for excessive celebration, Stanford kicked off from their twenty-five-yard line. Harmon squibbed the kickoff to reduce the possibility that Cal might return the kickoff for a touchdown. The squib wasn't sufficient. Thanks to five laterals, Cal's Kevin Moen took the ball into the end zone, where he met the Stanford marching band—which, assuming the game was over, had advanced onto the field—and ran over trombonist Gary Tyrrell.[1]

Prior to the kickoff, Cal announcer Joe Starkey remarked, "Only a miracle can save the [California] Bears now."

The American Heritage Dictionary defines a miracle as "An event that appears inexplicable by the laws of nature and so is held to be supernatural in origin or an act of God."

Nothing about "The Play" could be considered supernatural; the famous return took place entirely according to the laws of nature.[2] But in the eyes of many, the game-winning fiasco was nonetheless miraculous: "The Play," though not inexplicable, was certainly unexpected and unlikely. Most viewers, among them the members of the Stanford band, had assumed that Stanford had won the game when Harmon's kick went through the uprights with four seconds remaining. Most assumed that Stanford was headed to the Hall of Fame Bowl. "The Play," in a matter of seconds, changed an outcome that seemed inevitable.

THIN PLACES

Miracles are the subject of some of the most memorable Gospel narratives. Sunday school children learn about Jesus healing the blind beggar with an ointment made of saliva and dirt; forgiving the sins of the paralytic before restoring the man's ability to walk; changing water into wine at the wedding in Cana; and bringing Lazarus back to life after the young man had spent four days in the tomb. Sunday school teachers tell the story of Daniel surviving in the lions' den (Dan. 6), of God parting the sea for the Israelites who were fleeing captivity in Egypt (Exod. 13:17–14:31), and of the widow whose seemingly limited supply of oil and flour never ran out (1 Kings 17:7–24).

For children, these miracle stories serve as illustrations of God's love, might, and providence. They show that God is not bound by the limitations that humans take for granted. But as children grow into adolescents, doubts arise. Many young people who have been schooled in the Bible's many stories of God and God's people breaking the laws of physics and biology ask why they have not experienced or heard of similar miracles. Do miracles, such as those that God performed through Moses and Elijah and Jesus's disciples, still happen? If not, why?

A simple Internet search reveals several stories of current-day miracles, primarily involving recoveries from seemingly terminal illnesses or debilitating injuries. In addition to the obvious question of whether these seemingly miraculous events have rational, scientific explanations, such stories raise a difficult question: Why does God choose to miraculously heal some while others suffer or die?

Miracles certainly muddy the theological waters. Why would God make exceptions to the laws of nature that benefit some but not others? If miracles are possible, why doesn't God miraculously intervene to stop genocide, famine, or devastating natural disasters? These questions are beyond the scope of this book. But we can say with some certainty that, for reasons known only to God, miracles are generally not mechanisms for substantially changing the way things are. Jesus healed a blind man; he did not eliminate maladies that cause blindness. We sometimes hear stories of individuals whose cancer seems to have miraculously gone into remission; we don't hear stories of a type of cancer being mysteriously stricken from the face of the earth.

Perhaps miracles are glimpses of hope and reminders of what is possible. Maybe they are small signs that, despite the obvious brokenness and strife in our world, God is still in charge. Miracles show us that "for God all things are possible" (Matt. 19:26).

Ancient Celtic Christians used the term "thin places" to describe places and moments in which God is uniquely or especially present. Scholar and theologian Marcus Borg says that this Celtic way of thinking "affirms that there are . . . two layers or dimensions of reality, the visible world of our ordinary experience and God, the sacred, Spirit."[3] Borg explains, "'Thin places' are places where these two levels of reality meet or intersect. They are places where the boundary between the two levels becomes very soft, porous, permeable. Thin places are places where the veil momentarily lifts, and we behold

God."[4] Miracles are such "thin places" in which the veil lifts and we behold God more completely.

MIRACLES: IN MUSIC CITY AND ON THE ICE

In January of 2000 I witnessed a miracle on my parents' television set. With less than two minutes remaining in an AFC Wild Card Playoff game, the Tennessee Titans kicked a field goal to take a 15–13 lead over the Buffalo Bills. The Bills responded, driving down the field to score a field goal of their own. (On the final two plays of this scoring drive, Buffalo quarterback Rob Johnson played with only one shoe.) With only sixteen seconds on the clock the Bills went ahead of the Titans 16–15.

On the ensuing kickoff, Titans fullback Lorenzo Neal caught the ball and handed it to tight end Frank Wycheck. As the Bills kicking unit converged on Neal and Wycheck, Wycheck threw a lateral pass across the field to wide receiver Kevin Dyson, who ran seventy-five yards for a touchdown. The Titans won the game 22–16. (To this day some bitter Buffalo Bills fans contend that Wycheck's throw to Dyson was an illegal forward pass and that the play should not have been allowed to stand. For the purposes of this book, I will assume that these fans are wrong and that the officials were right to let the play stand.)

This incredible kickoff return is known in Tennessee and in football circles as the Music City Miracle. (As of this writing there is a web community of Titans fans known as Music City Miracles, www.musiccitymiracles.com.) While the Music City Miracle has special significance to me as a Titans fan, it was by no means the first or most memorable instance in which the word "miracle" was used to describe a sporting event. In fact the word is so commonly used to discuss the U.S. hockey team's performance at the 1980 Olympics in Lake Placid, New York, that the 2004 movie on the subject was simply titled *Miracle*. The team's victory over the Soviets in the semifinal of the medal round, which I discuss elsewhere in this book, certainly was outside the bounds of what most people considered possible. As the clock ran out with the United States leading the U.S.S.R. 4–3, ABC sportscaster Al Michaels asked his viewing audience (many of whom were, unfortunately, watching the game on tape delay[5]), "Do you believe in miracles?" Before long the phrase "Miracle on Ice" entered the cultural lexicon, and for nearly thirty years Americans have casually used the word "miracle" to describe a hockey game. (A satirical sports website once ran an article joking about the Vatican's refusal to recognize the Miracle on Ice as a bona fide miracle.[6])

The Los Angeles Dodgers won the National League pennant in 1988 behind the leadership of NL Most Valuable Player Kirk Gibson. Then they won the World Series with the help of Gibson's miracle home run. Heading into the series against the Oakland Athletics, however, Gibson had two injured legs and a stomach virus. No one expected him to play in the series. But in Game 1, with the Dodgers trailing 4–3 with two outs and one runner on base in the bottom of the ninth, Gibson hobbled to the plate to face future Hall-of-Fame relief pitcher Dennis Eckersley. Manager Tommy Lasorda had called on Gibson to pinch hit in one, last desperate attempt to win the game. Eck threw two strikes past Gibson, then two balls. Gibson fouled off the next pitch, and then the count went full when Eck threw ball three while the runner stole second base. Gibson swung at the seventh pitch of the at-bat and knocked it over the right field wall. Gibson found himself in a situation so often manufactured in backyards and sandlots. Despite being injured and ill, he came through in a big way with a miraculous game-winning home run.

Other sports miracles might include Reggie Miller scoring eight points in nine seconds to give the Pacers a victory over the Knicks in the 1995 NBA Playoffs[7]; UCLA's Tyus Edny going coast to coast to hit a last-second layup that would lift the Bruins over Missouri in the Sweet Sixteen of the 1995 NCAA Tournament; Doug Flutie's last-second, forty-eight-yard touchdown pass to Gerard Phelan, giving Boston College the win over rival Miami; and the Pittsburgh Steelers' Franco Harris catching a Terry Bradshaw touchdown pass that had bounced off a defender in the waning seconds of a 1972 playoff game against the Oakland Raiders. While none of these moments have miracle-themed nicknames, many fans and analysts use religious terminology to describe the latter two. Flutie's pass was an example of a Hail Mary, a long forward pass thrown in the final seconds of a game or half that has little chance of being completed. The name of the play alludes to the Roman Catholic prayer ritual in which one asks the Virgin Mary to intercede on one's behalf and was first used by Dallas Cowboys quarterback Roger Staubach to describe a "Hail Mary" pass he threw to win a 1975 playoff game against the Minnesota Vikings. The Bradshaw-to-Harris play would come to be known as the Immaculate Reception, a play on "Immaculate Conception," the Roman Catholic dogma that says that the Virgin Mary was conceived without the stain of original sin. (You can read more about the Hail Mary and the Immaculate Reception in the glossary of Religiously Inspired Sports Nicknames and Terminology in Appendix B of this book.)

Many of these miraculous moments have become the stuff of legend. These are the sorts of games and plays that people don't forget. They are the moments that sportscasters and columnists refer back to for years to come. They are the stories that we might not believe if we had not seen them on film.

BECAUSE I'VE SEEN IT BEFORE

Using the word "miracle" to describe a play on the football field or the performance of a hockey team may seem trite. Surely carrying a football for seventy-five yards without being tackled is not in the same league as restoring the life of a recently deceased son of a widow (1 Kings 17:17–24), feeding a multitude with five loaves of bread and two fish (Matt. 9:27–31), or healing a beggar who had been lame since birth (Acts 3:1–10). The casual use of the word "miracle" in the sports world threatens to cheapen the exploits of biblical miracle workers. But maybe the Music City Miracle can give us some perspective on the raising of the widow's son or the feeding of the five thousand.

Seeing the Music City Miracle or "The Play" or Flutie's Hail Mary—whether live or in highlights several years after the fact—changes the way in which one approaches football. After witnessing such "miraculous" plays, one can no longer assume that a game is over if a team trails by four or five points with only seconds remaining on the clock. As long as the team that is behind has possession of the ball or will gain possession by returning a kick, that team has the potential to score a touchdown and win the game. It has happened before, and it can happen again. The same thing applies in basketball. When I went to basketball games as a kid with my father, he used to tell me about the time the basketball team at his alma mater, Beech Grove High School in metropolitan Indianapolis, overcame a twenty-point deficit with two minutes to go to beat county rival Speedway High School. This, of course, was prior to the introduction of the three-point shot, making the feat all the more impressive. That story has kept me from turning off or walking out on many basketball games that appeared to have been decided with two minutes remaining. Even if my team is down by more than twenty points, I figure that the three-point shot allows for a few points above the Beech Grove–Speedway precedent. (If my team is trailing by thirty or more with 120 seconds remaining, I feel that I'm safe turning off the television.) Similarly, anyone who has watched a baseball team come back in the ninth inning after being down by several runs knows that there is some truth to the adage "It's not over until it's over" (commonly attributed to the great Yankees catcher Yogi Berra).

Fans and players can draw hope from these miraculous moments when their team is trailing with two outs in the ninth or when their team only has time to run one more play and needs a touchdown to win. "Maybe our guy will do what Kirk Gibson did in '88." "Maybe our guy will pull a Flutie out of his helmet." "If Beech Grove did it, we can do it." (Conversely, these realities should prevent us from assuming that our team's lead in the waning moments of a game is always sure to be safe—but I prefer to focus on the positive.)

John's Gospel describes Jesus's miracles as signs. Unlike Jesus's miracles in other Gospels, which are sometimes performed in secret and are not intended to draw attention to Jesus himself, his signs in John are public and done for the purpose of making believers. John 2:23 says, "When [Jesus] was in Jerusalem during the Passover festival, many believed in his name because they saw the signs that he was doing"; in 4:48 Jesus tells a royal official in Capernaum, "Unless you see signs and wonders you will not believe." For Christians, believing in Jesus as Messiah and Savior and God incarnate means believing in a redeemed and transformed creation—a creation in which the last are first and the first last (Matt. 20:16); in which people are free from poverty and oppression (Luke 4:18); in which the blind receive sight and the lame walk (Matt. 11:4–5); in which the old barriers of ethnicity and social status are meaningless (Gal. 3:28); and in which death and pain are no more (Rev. 21:4). Jesus's miracles (whether in John or in another Gospel), along with the miracles performed by prophets and apostles throughout the Scriptures, are signs that point to what God is doing and give us a glimpse of God's new creation fully realized.

Because of a miracle known as "The Play" we know that a football game can be won even by a team that is receiving the ball with only four seconds remaining. Similarly, because of the miracle of Jesus feeding a multitude with a few loaves and fishes, we know that God will provide for us and is capable of ending hunger. Because Jesus healed a Centurion's servant (Matt. 8:5–13) and exorcised a demon from the daughter of a Syrophoenician woman (Mark 7:24–30), we know that God is concerned with the health and well-being of God's children and that God's grace is not limited to a certain nation or ethnic group. Because Jesus miraculously gave life to the deceased, and he himself rose from the grave, we know that God is more powerful than death and that death will not have the final say.

PLAY HARD AS LONG AS YOU'RE IN THE GAME

Miracles not only give us knowledge of or belief in what is possible; they also inspire us to act. Any athlete who has seen a miraculous last-second play, comeback, or upset knows better than to quit even when the chances of winning seem remote. Even in these contests that appear out of reach, the best players give their best effort for as long as their coaches keep them in the game because they know there's a chance to make a comeback. They know that miracles are possible. The defensive side of a football team, when trailing by seven points with the clock winding down, will do anything in their power to make sure that their team gets another shot on offense. Even if the offense gets the ball on its own ten-yard line with sixteen seconds remaining, the opportunity is worth the effort. Miraculous finishes have happened before, and they can happen again.

In the face of overwhelming realities such as poverty, hunger, sickness, and materialism, Christians must take on the attitude of a linebacker in the final minute of a football game trying to give his offense one more shot. Even if a situation appears dire or hopeless, we should persist with the knowledge that God is capable of extraordinary and miraculous things and has a track record of working miracles in the interest of feeding the hungry and healing the sick. Most significantly, God is capable of bringing life out of death, proving to a skeptical world that hope is never lost and that nothing is impossible. We must continue doing God's work because we know the type of work that God is capable of doing.

11

"WE COULD ALWAYS TALK ABOUT BASEBALL"
Loving to Tell the Story

Who doesn't love a good sports movie?
You know, the kind that makes you want to stand up and cheer
for the athletes and teams who overcome huge challenges—
and learn important lessons along the way.

—BELIEFNET.COM

Keep these words that I am commanding you today in your heart.
Recite them to your children and talk about them when you are at home
and when you are away, when you lie down and when you rise.

—DEUTERONOMY 6:6

AT THE WATER COOLER

The best way to introduce the role of storytelling in sports would be to listen in on the proverbial "water-cooler conversations" that take place after notable sporting events. Here are some snippets from hypothetical water cooler conversations, some of which are based in part on actual conversations I've overheard or participated in. I've numbered these so that you can guess what sporting event is the subject of each one. Then check your answers with the key in appendix D. Some of these should be easy because they've been mentioned earlier in this book. (Because I'm emulating impromptu chit-chat, these stories are replete with hyperbole.)

1. "They weren't supposed to win that game. They weren't even supposed to be in that game. They were an eight seed. They were maybe the fourth best team in their own conference. Georgetown was the number one team in the country; they were the defending national champions; they had Ewing. No one was supposed to beat them. But when you shoot 80 percent from the field, I guess you can beat anybody."

2. "He wasn't supposed to play. He was injured. The announcers didn't see him anywhere—they didn't think he was even with the team. But the Dodgers were down in the ninth with two outs and Lasorda sent him in as a pinch hitter. He got down in the count 0–2, and with Eck on the mound, you figured it was over. But he stuck with it and, before you knew it, it was a full count. So you're thinking, 'Maybe they're not dead yet.' Then, the very next pitch, he knocks the ball over the right field fence. Game over."

3. "Perfection. A perfect 10. No one has ever done that before. At least not in the Olympics. She did it seven times and took home three gold medals. And she's only fourteen years old."

4. "They should always make the last stage a time trial. That was incredible. He was like a minute behind Fignon going into the last day, but he caught him. Caught him by eight seconds. Closest finish ever. And did you know that he hadn't even raced for two years because his brother-in-law shot him in a hunting accident?"

5. "Maybe you should pay attention to women's basketball. There's this tiny all-girls college in Philly that's beating everybody. They're about to win their third straight title. They've got this coach, Cathy Rush, whose putting to rest every negative stereotype of women's

basketball. Her teams are physical. They press; they set picks; they run up and down the floor. It's great."

6. "A year ago he was bagging groceries for minimum wage. Now he's the Super Bowl MVP. He didn't just make the team or get a chance to start or make the Pro Bowl—he did all three and he won the Super Bowl."

7. "They were a bunch of scrubs—amateurs. They didn't even belong on the ice with the Soviets. That Soviet team shut out an NHL all-star squad and beat Japan 16–0. The Soviets took an early lead, but our guys stuck with it. They kept coming back and coming back and eventually took the lead in the third period. Then they held on to win. It may have been the biggest upset in sports history. Let's just hope they can beat Finland and win the gold."

OR AT THE MOVIES

Another way to introduce this chapter would be to remind you of some of the sports stories that have inspired or been the basis for great American films. Here is a short, and admittedly incomplete, list, arranged alphabetically. Although there are many discrepancies between these films and the true stories on which they are based, the summaries describe both the films and the actual events.):

Brian's Song: Brian Piccolo and Gale Sayers, two young players for the Chicago Bears, become close friends and roommates despite being in a heated competition for the starting running back position. Piccolo helps Sayers recover from a knee injury, even though that knee injury gives Piccolo the starting job. The two grow especially when Piccolo is diagnosed with cancer and faces an early death at the age of twenty-six.

Chariots of Fire: British sprinters Harold Abrahams and Eric Liddell develop a rivalry in the 100 meter race leading up to the 1924 Olympic Games. But Liddell, because of his Christian faith, refuses to run in the race because it will be held on a Sunday. Teammate Andrew Lindsay offers to take Liddell's place in the 100 and allows Liddell to take Lindsay's place in the 400. Liddell wins the 400. Meanwhile Abrahams, who is Jewish and has fought anti-Semitism to earn the respect of his peers, wins the 100.

Cool Runnings: Under the tutelage of an American coach, a team of Jamaican sprinters and pushcart racers qualify for the four-man bobsled event in the 1988 Winter Olympics in Calgary. The Jamaicans are surprisingly competitive, but their sled breaks during the team's final run. The team shows extraordinary fortitude by carrying the sled across the finish line.

A League of Their Own: Because of the large numbers of young men required to fight World War II, Major League Baseball is threatened by instability. An enterprising baseball owner starts the All-American Girls Professional Baseball League to satisfy baseball fans while many of the best male players are overseas.

Miracle: University of Minnesota hockey coach Herb Brooks gets the job of coaching the United States hockey team in the 1980 Olympics in Lake Placid and assembles a team of unknown college players and amateurs to take on a field of more talented and experienced teams, including a Soviet team that had defeated several NHL teams in exhibition games (including a shut-out victory over a team of NHL All-Stars). After pulling off some surprises in Olympic group play, the team advances to the medal round, where they meet the heavily favorite Soviets in the semifinals. The rag-tag American team upsets the Soviets—against the backdrop of the Cold War, the Soviet invasion of Afghanistan, and a struggling American economy—and goes on to win the gold medal.

Our Lady of Victory: Twenty-three-year-old Cathy Rush is hired to coach the basketball team at Immaculata College, a tiny, all-women's school outside of Philadelphia, despite having no prior coaching experience. Without a recruiting budget, a travel budget, or even a gym, she assembles a team that wins three consecutive national championships.[1]

Remember the Titans: African American Coach Herman Boone takes over as head football coach at newly integrated T. C. Williams High School in 1971 Alexandria, Virginia. White coach Bill Yoast, who had been the head coach at Williams, is relegated to an assistant coaching position. Initially Yoast is reluctant to accept the role, but Boone and Yoast soon learn to work together to unite the team's white and black players. The T. C. Williams Titans are able to overcome prejudice and resentment (both from within and from outside) to win the state championship.

Rudy: Despite being undersized for a college football player and struggling in school due to dyslexia, Daniel "Rudy" Reuttiger is accepted into Notre Dame and earns a spot on the football team's practice squad as a walk-on. During the final game of Rudy's senior season Coach Dan Devine gives him a spot on the varsity squad. Rudy enters the game during the final defensive series and sacks the opposing quarterback. His teammates carry him off the field, making Rudy the first Notre Dame player ever to be honored in such a way.

Seabiscuit: A horse owner who hasn't recovered from the death of his son, an unassuming and unconventional trainer, a struggling and unheralded jockey, and an undersized and temperamental racehorse named Seabiscuit win several races and set several records during the mid-1930s. The pinnacle of Seabiscuit's career is a victory over Triple-Crown winner War Admiral. Seabiscuit becomes a symbol of hope to depression-era America.

The American Film Institute's 2005 list "100 Years . . . 100 Cheers: America's Most Inspiring Movies" includes several sports-related films, some based on true stories and some entirely fictional. *Rocky* (ranked fourth), *Breaking Away* (eighth), and *Hoosiers* (thirteenth) all rank in the top fifteen.[2] For a more complete list of inspirational sports movies, see "Appendix C: A Dictionary of Inspirational Sports Movies."

Sports are a great subject for film both because most sports are, by their nature, visual and action-packed, and because the sports world has produced so many great stories. These are stories about the triumph of the human will, about overcoming adversity, and about relationships that develop among athletes devoted to a common goal. These are stories in which the stakes are always high even though the only thing on the line is the outcome of a game or race.

WHEN A GAME IS MORE THAN JUST A GAME

Sports fans love to tell stories. They love to relive game-changing plays and to recount the achievements of athletes who have overcome great odds. They enjoy talking to other people who saw the big game and catching up those who missed it. They draw hope and inspiration from tales of teams whose commitment and determination and unity lift them above more esteemed competition. They get chills recalling how they witnessed history on the football field or the baseball diamond or the tennis court (or through the television set).

The best sportscasters are storytellers. All-time greats such as Red Barber, Mel Allen, Vin Scully, Jack Buck, Chick Hearn, Al Michaels, and Jim Nantz not only explain, with an economy of words, what is happening, but why it is significant. They explain what is at stake and let their listeners and viewers know when a game is more than just a game (or a home run is more than just a home run or a putt is more than just a putt.) Michaels, in Lake Placid in 1980, didn't say during the final seconds of the semifinal contest between the U.S. and Soviet hockey teams, "The Americans win 4–3 and will advance to play for the gold medal." Instead he asked the now famous rhetorical question, "Do you believe in miracles?" He took his viewers to the climax of an incredible story, a story of overcoming great odds during a time of unrest and uncertainty.

Likewise, sports news is at its best when it tells the stories behind the games, matches, and races it covers. ESPN's flagship news program *SportsCenter* is successful largely because of its ability to tell a good story. This is true not only of personal interest stories, such as a segment on an autistic teen who was given a chance to play in the final minutes of a high school basketball game and scored twenty points (including six three-pointers),[3] or the college football player who obtained legal guardianship of his little brother to rescue the younger sibling from an unstable home life,[4] but also of stories about otherwise ordinary contests. SportsCenter puts games in context, drawing attention to recent or long-standing rivalries between teams or coaches, a player returning to face the team that released him, or a historical trend that has been suspended. When Duke and North Carolina's men's basketball teams face off, SportsCenter reviews the entire history of the rivalry—the greatest players and moments, the most meaningful games, the most incredible finishes—and presents the game as one more chapter in this ongoing saga (a chapter in which an Atlantic Coast Conference championship or a top seed in the NCAA tournament may be on the line). When Tiger Woods is leading going into the final day of one of the PGA's four major tournaments, SportsCenter reminds viewers that Woods (as of this writing, anyway) never loses when he is leading going into the final eighteen holes of a major, and explains how winning this tournament will put Woods one step closer to breaking Jack Nicklaus's record of eighteen major titles.

Sarah Arthur, in *The God-Hungry Imagination*, writes, "Story has staying power. We remember the illustrations from Sunday's sermon for months afterward, but by coffee hour we're already struggling to recite the pastor's three main points."[5] She adds, "Story incarnates meaning, embodies content, rather than confronting the hearer's reason with propositional argument."[6] In the case of sports one might say that story incarnates meaning and embodies content instead of confronting the hearer with statistics and "coachspeak." The fact that Lance Armstrong finished the 1999 Tour de France in ninety-one hours, thirty-two minutes, sixteen seconds is trivial. The story of Armstrong surviving cancer and coming back to win the world's most famous and most grueling bicycle race is inspirational. Likewise, no one would care that someone named Daniel Reuttiger[7] recorded one sack for Notre Dame during the 1975 season were it not for Reuttiger's story of being an undersized walk-on who worked relentlessly to realize his lifelong dream. If not for the stories of curses, failure, and never living up to the standard set by the rival Yankees, the 2004 Red Sox would eventually be no more significant than the 1930 Philadelphia Athletics or the 1983 Baltimore Orioles or any other World Series winner that casual fans largely have forgotten. Story makes sports matter.

"WE COULD ALWAYS TALK ABOUT BASEBALL"

In the 1991 movie *City Slickers*, three men from New York City go on a cattle-driving vacation to escape the pressures of day-to-day life. At one point the three lead characters are debating their generation's best right fielder when Bonnie, one of their fellow vacationers, scoffs at their obsession with baseball. Bonnie explains that she likes baseball and enjoys going to the occasional game, but she can't understand why so many people (and especially men) talk about the sport so incessantly. One of the men, Phil, explains that when he was a teenager, he and his father couldn't talk about much of anything, but they could always talk about baseball.[8] In his own way Phil illustrates Sarah Arthur's point when she writes, "Story creates a connection between the teller and the hearer(s). . . . Somehow the narrator is giving of himself or herself in deeper and more vulnerable ways than in regular discourse."[9]

Storytelling is the means by which new generations of fans are born and by which fathers and mothers (and grandfathers, grandmothers, aunts, uncles, and so forth) pass on their love of a sport or team to their children. Most of the Boston Red Sox fans who celebrated the team's 2004 and 2007 World Series victories were too young to have had first-hand experience of much of the team's infamous eighty-six years of futility. But they knew the stories. They knew about the Curse of the Bambino; they knew about Bucky Dent's heart-breaking home run in 1978; they knew about the team's close calls in the 1975 and 1986 World Series. Through the power of story, these fans have claimed their team's past struggles as their own. Those who were raised to be fans of Notre Dame football likewise know the stories of Knute Rockne, the Gipper, Rudy, and the school's seven Heisman Trophy winners and eleven consensus national championships. Despite Notre Dame's recent struggles on the football field and its inability to win a bowl game, storytelling enables young fans of the Fighting Irish to feel a connection to one of the great programs in college football history.

Some of my fondest memories from my early adolescence involve going to high school basketball games or driving to Bloomington to watch the Indiana Hoosiers. These experiences were especially meaningful because I knew the stories of tiny Milan High School's unlikely title run, Oscar Robertson and the great team from Crispus Attucks High School that became the first team from an all-black high school to win a state championship (in any state), and the time Beech Grove High School overcame a twenty-point deficit with two minutes remaining to beat Speedway; I heard tales about Kent Benson and Quinn Buckner and Indiana's perfect season in 1976 and how Isiah Thomas led the Hoosiers to the 1981 NCAA championship.

Our tickets to Indiana University basketball games put us in Assembly Hall's upper balcony, so far above the action that it was hard to keep track of which player had the ball without binoculars. The height gave me an excellent view of the several-stories-high championship banners that hung at either end of the court. I knew the stories behind many of them. I knew that I had (so the story goes) cheered for the 1976 championship team from my mother's belly. I knew that Landon Turner, one of the stars of the 1981 championship team, had a severe car accident a few months after the title game that left him paralyzed from the chest down. The Boston Celtics drafted him anyway in 1982 as a goodwill gesture. (Turner was on his way to King's Island, a Cincinnati-area amusement park that my friends and I frequented during our high school and college years, when he had the accident. Whenever I went to King's Island, my dad made sure to remind me of Landon Turner.) I knew that back in 1979, when Indiana won the National Invitational Tournament (NIT), the NIT still meant something.[10] I knew that Steve Alford, hero of the 1987 championship team, was a coach's son who had played at New Castle High School, home to the largest high school gymnasium in the world.

Hinkle Fieldhouse on the campus of Butler University played host to the regional and semistate portions of the Indiana High School Athletic Association (IHSAA) basketball tournament. During the late 1980s and early 1990s several future college and pro players, such as Alan Henderson and Eric Montross, came through Hinkle during the tournament. But Hinkle is perhaps best known for having hosted the IHSAA finals from 1928 until 1971. Hinkle was where Milan's Bobby Plump hit a last-second jumper to upset powerhouse Muncie Central. It was where Oscar Robertson led Attucks High School to back-to-back titles. It was where future Indiana University greats Jimmy Rayl and the VanArsdale twins fell just short, losing in the title game. It was where *Hoosiers* was filmed.

The stories made Hinkle and Assembly Hall holy ground for Indiana basketball fans. Stories gave our trips to these hoops shrines greater significance and strengthened the bond between father and son. My experience with my father growing up was much more positive than that of Phil in *City Slickers*. But on the rare occasion that we were having a rough time, we could still always talk about basketball.

Today, I spend much of my Sunday afternoons on the phone with my parents and my sister. (I should note that, during the football season, "Sunday afternoon" starts at about 3:00 when the Titans game is over.) Almost without exception, sports talk dominates my phone conversations with my father and sister. We tell stories about games we saw or read about or heard about. These stories are parts of bigger stories. The story of Vanderbilt's unlikely victory over Auburn and ascent into the national rankings is part of the larger story of Vanderbilt being the doormat of the Southeastern Conference and struggling to achieve their first winning season in more than two decades. The story of Reggie Miller's farewell speech to Pacers fans at Conseco Fieldhouse is part of the larger story of how Reggie—by his swagger and by his clutch shooting—carried the Pacers from the margins of the NBA into the latter rounds of the playoffs. Without the larger narratives, the story of a team winning a regular season game or of a player retiring isn't terribly meaningful.

WE LOVE TO TELL THE STORY

Christians, perhaps even more than sports fans, are a people of story. Storytellers likely passed down tales of faith heroes such as Abraham and Sarah and Jacob and Moses orally for generations before these stories were written on scrolls. The biblical stories of Joseph, Ruth, and Esther, with their plot twists and complex characters, read like novellas. The Book of Job is an epic poem. Jesus taught in parables—short, fictional stories that illustrate an important point about God and God's relationship to humanity. The Bible, in addition to being a collection of stories, is itself a grand narrative of God's creation and redemption of the world.

In the words of Katherine Hankey's well-known hymn, Christians "love to tell the story."[11] Sure, few Christians sit around at family gatherings recalling the exploits of Deborah, David, or Paul. Even fewer gather at the water cooler and say to one another, "Hey. Did you hear about those three guys who survived the fiery furnace?" And we don't tend to call our fellow Christians minutes after hearing a great sermon to say, "You won't believe this . . . ." Christians generally use different methods than sports fans to tell the stories of God's love for creation. (Then again, stories from the Scriptures, much like stories from the sports world, seem to translate well to film.)

The Christian calendar is perhaps the church's primary storytelling medium. The Christian year begins with Advent and the preparation for the coming of Christ. It continues through Christ's birth at Christmas and the visit of the magi at Epiphany. During the ensuing season Christians celebrate Jesus's baptism and transfiguration. Lent takes the church on a long, and sometimes painful, journey to Jerusalem, culminating with Jesus's death on Good Friday. Easter is a celebration of Christ's resurrection and the beginning of a season of new hope and new life. Pentecost recalls the birth of the church and the pouring out of the Holy Spirit. Lectionary readings supplement and accentuate the Christian calendar and the story it tells. The Revised Common Lectionary used in worship by many mainline Protestants in North America tells the Christian story three different ways in each of three years, each year using a different combination of scriptures. The lectionary lifts up a variety of stories from the Bible, each of which is an important piece of God's grand narrative.

Lectionary readings are one of many ways in which Christians tell our story during worship. The lighting of candles reminds us that Christ is the light of the world, a light that darkness cannot overcome. (See John 1:1–5; 8:12.) The hymns and songs of praise that we sing recall many aspects of God's story. The baptismal liturgy uses water to tell the story of how God claims us and cleanses us—through creation, the flood, the crossing of the Red Sea, Jesus's baptism, and Jesus's command to go forth and baptize others. Holy Communion tells the story of Jesus's final evening with his closest disciples and recalls his command to "Do this in remembrance of me" (Luke 22:19).

Just as sports fans take their stories beyond the stadiums, arenas, and living rooms where they gather in mutual appreciation of the games they love, Christians take our story beyond the walls of the sanctuary. Christians gather for Bible study in coffee shops and restaurants; they sit around fires at summer camps to tell stories and sing songs about the heroes of the faith. Many leaders in the church spend a few years in seminary where they hone their storytelling skills (in a manner of speaking).

An important aspect of Christian storytelling is passing on the story to the next generations. When sports fans know the stories of the teams they follow, they better understand the significance of each game and become more fully invested in the team's successes and failures. Likewise, when young Christians know their story, they gain an appreciation and understanding of Christian values and practices. They realize that they belong to something much larger than themselves and that they are connected to millions of other Christians, past, present, and future. Arthur writes, "Without story to engage the imagination, there's no sense of a narratable structure (beginning, middle, and end) that connects a young person to the wider world."[11] If the church is to thrive, it must provide a "narratable structure" to its children and youth. Through worship, Sunday school, camps and retreats, mission trips and service projects, and numerous other ministry settings, the church must explain to young people, "This is who we are; this is how we came to be; and this is how we must live as a result." Otherwise everything that Christians do and everything that Christians value will have no meaning to new generations of Christians.

Consider Boise State's upset of Oklahoma in the Fiesta Bowl on New Year's Day 2007. One could not fully appreciate the significance of that game without knowing the story behind it. Sure, any football fan could marvel at the litany of trick plays that Boise State ran in the fourth quarter and overtime, but the story of that game was much larger than what happened on the field on January 1, 2007. Without knowing the story, one might not be surprised that Boise State, an undefeated team (albeit from a lesser conference), defeated a two-loss Oklahoma team. The larger story includes the rich tradition of Oklahoma Sooners football—a program that had won several national championships and had been a member of one of college football's most prestigious conferences, the Big 12 (formerly known as the Big 8, Big 7, and Big 6), since the conference's inception. In the seven years leading up to the game Oklahoma had played in three National Championship Games, winning one; the Sooners had also won the 2003 Rose Bowl. The Boise State Broncos, by contrast, had never played in one of the major bowl games and played in a conference that (in its current configuration) had never sent a team to a major bowl game. Boise State didn't even begin play in Division I-A (currently Division I-FBS), the highest classification in college football, until 1996. While Oklahoma was winning its first national title in 1950, Boise State was a junior college unknown outside Idaho. The 2007 Fiesta Bowl was the climax of a story about an upstart college football program stunning one of the sport's most storied teams on one of the game's biggest stages. It was an important chapter in the story about great football being played outside of the power conferences by teams not named Oklahoma or Ohio State or USC or Alabama.

Similarly the Christian story gives greater significance to our rituals and sacraments and our common values. Apart from the larger story, Holy Communion is a simple worship ritual or a community meal. But those who know the story understand the setting in which Jesus first introduced this ritual, the connection between the Eucharist and the Passover meal celebrated by the ancient Israelites and their Jewish descendants, and the fact that for nearly two millennia Christians have faithfully broken bread and drunk wine in remembrance of the One who gave his life to deliver humanity from sin and death. Similarly the Christian story puts into context the church's emphasis on serving and seeking justice for others, especially those who are poor, sick, or somehow marginalized. God's chosen people suffered bondage and oppression in Egypt before enduring poverty and hunger in the wilderness. Thus God expected them to provide for the poor and the stranger. The Old Testament prophets reminded the people that God would hold them accountable for their treatment of the least among them. When Jesus stood in the synagogue in Nazareth at the beginning of his earthly ministry, he read from Isaiah 61, saying, "The Spirit of the Lord is upon me, because he has anointed me to bring good news to the poor. He has sent me to proclaim release to the captives and recovery of sight to the blind, to let the oppressed go free, to proclaim the year of the Lord's favor" (Luke 4:18-19). Jesus consistently reached out to those who were poor or ailing or who had been shunned by society. He told his followers that, by feeding the hungry and welcoming the stranger and visiting the prisoner, they were actually feeding and welcoming and visiting him. (See Matthew 25:31-46.)

ANY GOOD STORY DESERVES TO BE TOLD

Any good story demands to be told, whether on SportsCenter or in worship on the second Sunday in Advent. In sports and in the church, knowing the story gives greater meaning to what we see and experience. Stories tell us what matters and why, and the best stories invite readers and listeners to enter the narrative and make the story their own.

Sports broadcasters, writers, and fans have long been masterful storytellers, passing down tales of legendary players, teams, games, and seasons to subsequent generations. These stories give young fans a context in which to place the sports that they see and experience. As they fit their sporting moments into larger narratives, they become storytellers in their own right, capable of passing on their stories to the next generation.

The Christian church has a long and great history of storytelling that it would do well to embrace. By telling our incredible story of God's creation and redemption of the world, we pass down our beliefs, values, and identity to younger generations, thereby creating new storytellers who will carry and continue the story into the future.

12

TREATED LIKE GODS

Sports Obsession and Idolatry

In the absence of a shimmering skyline, the Odessas
of the country had all found something similar in which to place
their faith. In Indiana, it was the plink-plink-plink of a ball
on a parquet floor. In Minnesota, it was the swoosh of skates on
the ice. In Ohio and Pennsylvania and Alabama and
Georgia and Texas and dozens of other states, it was the
weekly event simply known as Friday Night.

—H. G. "BUZZ" BISSINGER, *FRIDAY NIGHT LIGHTS*

You shall not make for yourself an idol, whether in the
form of anything that is in heaven above, or that is on the
earth beneath, or that is in the water under the earth.
You shall not bow down to them or worship them.

—EXODUS 20:4–5A

THANK YOU FOR OUR VICTORIES; DELIVER US FROM DEFEAT

I teach the ninth- and tenth-grade Sunday school class at my United
Methodist congregation in Nashville. At the beginning of each Sunday
school hour, we gather with the students and teachers from the other

youth Sunday school classes to share joys and concerns. Without fail, several of these prayer requests are sports-related. Often, the person in charge of listing the joys and concerns on the whiteboard will simply write "sports" in between the joys column and the concerns column. Some of these sports-inspired prayer requests involve the teens' athletic endeavors, whether celebrations of success at the previous day's swim meet or concerns about an upcoming tryout. But many of these joys and concerns deal with the successes or failures of the students' favorite college and professional teams or superstar athletes. A big win for Vanderbilt's basketball team sits on the markerboard among the joys, next to a college acceptance letter or an opportunity to travel abroad. An unexpected Titans loss sits among the concerns next to genocide in Darfur or a family member's illness.

Sports are by no means outside the sphere of God's influence or blessing. God is with us on the athletic field or in the bleachers just as God is with us in the sanctuary, the workplace, or the classroom. While sports may seem out of place in the company of global crises, health concerns, and milestone achievements, athletics is by no means unworthy as a subject of prayer. On the other hand, we must take care that the sports we love and care about do not become an object of worship or a religion unto themselves.

PLAYING THE BLUES IN CHICAGO

Even the most devoted sports fans would likely confess that, in the grand scheme of things, sports really aren't all that important. Although the stakes appear to be high, the outcomes of most contests are largely insignificant. By and large, the lives, careers, and general well-being of sports fans are not tied to the success of their favorite teams. (The lives, careers, and general well-being of coaches who are under intense pressure to win at any cost are a different story. More on that later.) Millions of Cubs fans continue to live fulfilling lives despite their beloved team's century of struggles. Yet, the pain of a favorite team's failures and the exhilaration surrounding that team's success can, rightly or wrongly, have a very real effect on one's attitudes and emotions.

Cub-fan frustration got out of hand during Game 6 of the 2003 National League Championship Series. The Cubs were leading the

Florida Marlins 3–0 with one out in the top of the eighth inning. The Cubs led the series 3–2 and were five outs away from the World Series. Cubs ace Mark Prior was on the mound, and Marlins second baseman Luis Castillo was at the plate. Castillo hit a fly ball into foul territory in left field. Cubs left fielder Moises Alou ran after the ball to make the out. As Alou went for the ball, Steve Bartman, a fan in the front row, beat him to the catch, causing Alou to slam down his glove in frustration. Following the incident, the Marlins went on a run and won the game 8–3.

While analysts have debated whether Alou actually would have been able to make a play on the ball, many were nonetheless irate with Bartman and what they perceived as fan interference. Bartman endured verbal abuse (and physical abuse in the form of food and other things being thrown at him) as security escorted him from the stadium. Following the game, Alou said of the incident, "I timed it perfectly, I jumped perfectly. I'm almost 100 percent that I had a clean shot to catch the ball. All of a sudden, there's a hand on my glove."[1] Bartman became the subject of ridicule on Internet message boards, and Jeb Bush, then the governor of the Marlins' home state of Florida, jokingly offered the disgraced fan asylum in the Sunshine State. Since then Bartman, much like the billy goat (see chapter 1), has become synonymous with the Cubs' futility. According to a 2008 ESPN.com article, written more than four years after the infamous game, Bartman was still "in hiding" somewhere in the Chicago area.[2]

Steve Bartman's fellow fans made the game and the Cubs' narrative bigger than Bartman's dignity and well-being. Many forget that after the incident with the foul ball, the Cubs gave up four runs before making another out. All told, the Marlins scored eight runs in the remainder of the eighth inning, six of them unearned. Blaming Steve Bartman ignores an error by shortstop Alex Gonzalez on what could have been a double play to end the inning, and a walk and wild pitch by Prior. Moreover, Alou has since said that he wouldn't have caught the ball anyway.[3]

FIRE[ENTER YOUR COACH'S NAME HERE].COM

The Cubs fans who made Steve Bartman's life miserable are hardly alone in letting an obsession with a sports team have an impact on their treatment of or attitude toward fellow human beings. Just days after the

University of Florida hired Ron Zook as head football coach, replacing coaching legend Steve Spurrier, who had decided to coach in the NFL, a fan set up the website www.fireronzook.com. As Zook's team struggled in the coach's first year, the site garnered national attention and grew in popularity. After three disappointing seasons (albeit three seasons in which Florida had a winning record) the effort was successful, and Zook was out. I mention Zook because of the website, but several more successful coaches have been fired or forced to resign to appease dissatisfied fan bases. For instance, the NBA's Seattle Supersonics in 1998 fired George Karl after six consecutive seasons in which Karl's team won fifty-five or more games and finished first or second in its division. Karl's sin was his failure to win a championship. But after Karl was fired no Seattle team came close. (The franchise has since moved to Oklahoma City.) For years University of Michigan football fans called on the university to fire head coach Lloyd Carr. Carr's teams never had a losing season, were ranked nationally at the end of almost every season, and won a national title in 1997. Yet, Carr's teams had lost in the Rose Bowl too many times and had fallen to rival Ohio State too many times for fans to stomach. Carr resigned under pressure in 2007. In the first year under his successor, Rich Rodriguez, Michigan's football team went 3–9, losing more games than any team in Michigan football history. As of this writing, a Google search reveals that several Michigan fans are already calling for Rich Rodriguez's dismissal, among them the proprietor of www.firerrod.com.

Fans who call for a coach's head rarely consider the effect their vitriolic outbursts on talk radio and the Internet might have on the families and loved ones of the coach in question. When a college coach is under pressure, angry fans seldom consider the coach's relationship to the players as a mentor and teacher. They seldom think about player graduation rates during the coach's tenure. Too often all that matters is winning big games and winning championships at any cost.

OBSESSION AND IDOLATRY

Attacking a fan who unintentionally may or may not have altered the outcome of an important game and demanding that a coach be fired for failing to lead a team to a championship are symptoms of sports obsession. Obsession with sports is so common in North America that no one finds it strange when a family selects a paint color for their living room to match the color of their favorite college or professional team. (Glidden and Home Depot offer Team Colors paint to match every NFL, NHL, and Major League Soccer team, most major college athletic programs, and several top NASCAR drivers.) Nor do we think it absurd that someone would pay several hundred dollars for tickets to a highly anticipated match-up between two undefeated college football teams. Americans each year invest billions of dollars and billions of hours into their favorite teams and athletes. Some of the largest and most impressive structures in almost every major American city are stadiums and arenas that are used primarily for professional and college sports. Sports obsession is part of our culture. And in some cases our obsession with sports borders on idolatry.

The *American Heritage Dictionary* defines an idol as "One that is adored, often blindly or excessively."[4] Too often sports fans are guilty of making sports or teams into idols. Fans sometimes ascribe so much significance and importance to sports that their athletic obsessions distract them from more important matters such as family relationships and participation in a faith community.

The father who won't talk to his children while the big game is on television and the family that skips church because they have football tickets are American clichés. So is the teen who disappears from her church youth group because she spends every weekend playing in traveling tournaments. From an early age many North American children learn that sports are worthy of a devotion that is due few other pursuits. Youth minister Walt Mueller, in an article on the religion of sports among youth and their families, laments the "professionalization" of youth sports: "The youngest of the young experience sports that are organized for them complete with regular practices, fancy uniforms, expensive equipment, the best playing fields, arenas, coaches, paid officials, aggressive game schedules, out-of-state travel, and weekend tournaments."[5] Many youth pastors have remarked on the incredible ministries they would have if their teens were half as devoted to church as they were to sports.

Religious communities tend not to interfere with the cult of sports. Some even support it. One church in Madison, Wisconsin, for instance, moved its Sunday, January 20, 2008, service up an hour so that members would be able to worship without having to miss watching the Green Bay Packers play in the NFC Championship Game.[6] Many congregations host Super Bowl parties (though the NFL has recently argued that many such events violate the league's copyright[7]). Of course, church softball and basketball leagues are common throughout the United States.

Participating in a church softball league is hardly idolatrous. On the contrary, I applaud churches for creating an environment that fosters fun and friendly competition. But the fact that so many congregations sponsor sports teams and leagues says a lot about the place of athletics in our culture. We have a thirst for competition. Many who are young and fit seek ways to display their athletic prowess, whether through church, community, intramural, interscholastic, or professional leagues. Many more compete vicariously through their favorite college and professional teams and athletes. They boast about their favorite team defeating an archrival or winning a conference championship; they hang their heads when their team loses a close game or their favorite player chokes.

Such passion for sports is responsible for much unnecessary tension and anxiety and tends to distract people from more worthy pursuits. Setting aside a few hours on Saturday to watch the big game can be a healthy way to unwind—some might even consider it a form of sabbath rest. But when one ignores one's family and friends to focus on a sporting event (particularly when one is a spectator rather than a participant) and when one's mood for the remainder of the day or weekend depends on the outcome of said sporting event, sports has become an idol. A love of sports should not dictate one's attitude and behavior and it should not supersede one's relationships.

I confess that I am guilty of sports idolatry. The writing of this book was disrupted briefly when Vanderbilt's football team unexpectedly lost to Duke. A win over Duke would have given the Commodores six wins, making them eligible for their first bowl game since 1982. In the moments following the game, I avoided talking to my family. For the next week, I avoided all coverage of college football, a game I otherwise follow incessantly. I only grudgingly turned on ESPN's College Game Day the following Saturday. I was grumpy. Because of a football game. I had assigned irrational significance to a sporting event and allowed it to have undue influence on my attitude and behavior. I'd made Vanderbilt football into an idol.

THE CULT OF SPORT

In 1983 then Texas governor Mark White tapped billionaire H. Ross Perot to head a committee on educational reform. Perot was particularly critical of school systems that, in his view, poured too many resources into and put too much emphasis on extracurricular activities (read: sports). Among his targets was Permian High School in Odessa. Permian is, perhaps most famously, the subject of Buzz Bissinger's bestselling book *Friday Night Lights* and the inspiration for the subsequent motion picture and television series. In 1982 Permian had spent $5.6 million on its football stadium complete with a two-story press box and seating for more than nineteen thousand. Odessa residents were not happy with Perot's assessment and responded with a vigorous letter-writing campaign. Some of the letters "were addressed 'Dear Idiot' or something worse than that."[8] In *Friday Night Lights* Brad Allen, former president of the Permian booster club explains, "There are so few other things we can look at with pride. . . . When somebody talks about West Texas, they talk about football. There is nothing to replace it. It's an integral part of what made the community strong. You take it away and it's almost like you strip the identity of the people."[9]

The cult of high school basketball in many Indiana towns rivals the football obsession in Odessa and other parts of Texas. Indiana high schools boast many of the world's largest high school gymnasiums, and they make use of the capacity. When Anderson plays Anderson Highland, Anderson's nearly nine-thousand-seat Wigwam has standing room only, and even those who have seats are on their feet. Star players in small towns across the state become local heroes and household names, even if they never succeed on the college level. To quote Barbara Hershey's character, Myra Fleener, in *Hoosiers*, "You know, a basketball hero around here is treated like a god. . . . I've seen them, the real sad ones. They sit around the rest of their lives talking about the glory days when they were seventeen years old."[10] "Hoosier Hysteria" even has its own Wikipedia entry (though, as of this writing, it has been marked for needing cleanup and not citing references).

Bissinger in *Friday Night Lights* explains the obsession with high school sports in so many parts of the country. "In the absence of a shimmering skyline," he writes, "the Odessas of the country had all found something similar in which to place their faith. In Indiana, it was the plink-plink-plink of a ball on a parquet floor. In Minnesota, it was the swoosh of skates on the ice. In Ohio and Pennsylvania and Alabama and Georgia and Texas and dozens of other states, it was the weekly event simply known as Friday Night."[11]

Because of this obsession with high school sports in so many parts of the country, adults live vicariously through teenage athletes, many of whom are not yet legal adults, and allow the outcomes of adolescent competitions to disproportionately influence their mood. This obsession with high school athletics has been exacerbated by the emphasis on college recruiting, particularly in basketball and football. ESPN covers National Signing Day, the first day on which high school seniors can sign a National Letter of Intent saying that they will be attending a certain college. Services such as Scouts, Inc. and Rivals rank the nation's top high school basketball and football players and issue detailed reports on each player's skills and deficiencies and the universities he is considering. (I say "he" because neither service provides information on women's basketball.)

The most highly touted high school athletes are under intense pressure, both from outsiders and from themselves, to succeed. Some grow up in communities with a bloated sense of the importance of high school sports. Some are targeted by scouts and coaches who see in them the potential to play at the college or professional level. Some see success in sports as the only way to get a college education or lift their families out of poverty (and some feel intense pressure from their parents or guardians to do just that).

The 1994 documentary *Hoop Dreams* tells the story of Arthur Agee and William Gates, two Chicago-area high school basketball players who dreamed of playing in the NBA. Both Gates and Agee hailed from Chicago housing projects. Both players were recruited by St. Joseph's High School, an affluent Catholic school in Chicago's western suburbs that produced NBA all star and hall-of-famer Isiah Thomas. According to the film, when Agee and Gates entered St. Joseph's, both were at a fourth-grade academic level.

Gates demonstrated star power early on and was able to contribute to the varsity team as a freshman. St. Joseph's faculty went out of their way to make sure that Gates' tuition was covered and that his grades steadily improved. Agee, by contrast, was a project. He was relegated to the freshman team and when his family struggled to pay their portion of the tuition (half of the tuition was covered by scholarship), St. Joseph's kicked Agee out. Three years would pass before Agee received credit for the work he did at St. Joseph's. Agee finished his high school education at John Marshall High School, an inner-city public school on Chicago's west side, where he would eventually lead the basketball team to the final four of the Illinois high school basketball tournament.

Both teens had a close family member whose basketball dreams were never realized and who lived vicariously through the younger, more talented member of the household. For William Gates, this person was his brother Curtis, a former high school and junior college superstar whose academic struggles ended his career. For Arthur Agee, it was his father Bo, who had been a promising high school player before getting mixed up in drugs and crime. Curtis Gates worked several short-term, low-paying jobs; Bo Agee left the family and spent time in prison before having a religious conversion and returning home. Both felt that their past failures would be vindicated by William and Arthur's success on the basketball court, particularly if one of the two players were to have made it to the NBA. (Neither did, though Agee played semipro ball and Gates was offered a tryout with the Washington Wizards before fracturing a bone in his foot.[12]) Looking back on his high school days and lamenting not winning a championship, Bo Agee remarked on the eve of his son playing in the state finals, "Twenty-one years later I have a chance to get a championship through him."[13]

William Gates especially faced intense pressure from many sources: His brother was living a dream through him; his high school coach Gene Pingatore expected him to be an all-time great in the mold of Isiah Thomas; college coaches, scouts, and sports writers saw him as one of the nation's most promising basketball prospects; and Gates himself knew that he had the potential to one day play professionally. The pressure wore on Gates, and his interest in basketball waned during his junior and senior years of high school. Still, he knew that basketball had paid for his high school education and was his only means of attending college. He grew frustrated as Coach Pingatore encouraged him to "write off" concerns that didn't involve basketball, such as his relationship with his girlfriend and their infant son. William Gates wanted his life to be more than basketball, but all the opportunities that were available to him were basketball-related. In the film, Curtis Gates astutely described this tension saying, "When basketball is over, William might not have a friend in the world."[14]

Arthur Agee, when he was forced to leave the basketball hotbed of St. Joseph's High School, kept out of the spotlight and was able to develop at his own pace—at least where basketball was concerned. Unfortunately, because Agee wasn't a nationally ranked hoops prospect, few were clamoring to make sure that he kept his grades up or stayed out of trouble. Fortunately, Agee cut ties with a best friend who had gotten mixed up in gangs and drugs and was able to graduate and earn a basketball scholarship to a junior college. Agee would later play Division I ball at Arkansas State.

Today, both Agee and Gates live in the Chicago area. Gates earned a bachelor's degree from Marquette and is currently a pastor; Agee works to help inner-city teens attend college. Both live comfortably, largely because of basketball and because of *Hoop Dreams*. "Where would I be if 'Hoop Dreams' never happened?" Agee asked in a 2004 *Washington Post* article. "I don't know."[15] Both Curtis Gates[16] and Bo Agee,[17] whose basketball dreams never materialized, died prematurely, victims of violence in some of Chicago's poorest and roughest neighborhoods.

For Gates and Agee basketball was much more than a game, it was their hope—and in their minds possibly their only hope—for a better life. In the eyes of many, the value of these two athletes as human beings was determined largely by how they performed on the basketball court. Basketball became an idol, not necessarily to Gates and Agee, but to those relatives, coaches, and recruiters who had a stake in the two teens' hoops careers.

KEEPING THINGS IN PERSPECTIVE

As a lover of sports myself, I do not want to suggest that there is anything wrong with being a devoted fan or athlete. Playing sports, aside from the obvious benefits to one's physical health, is a great way to build relationships and learn important teamwork and leadership skills. Watching sports and cheering for a favorite team give us occasions to spend memorable moments with friends and family and can serve as a healthy distraction in times of sadness or anxiety. And, as I hope this book has demonstrated, sports can give us glimpses of how God is at work in the world. But we need to be careful to keep things in perspective.

The second commandment (for Protestants, the second half of the first commandment for Roman Catholics) says, "You shall not make for yourself an idol, whether in the form of anything that is in heaven above, or that is on the earth beneath, or that is in the water under the earth. You shall not bow down to them or worship them" (Exod. 20:4–5a). Few of us intend to make sports (or money or anything else) into an idol. But we fashion it into an idol when we allow it to have a greater influence on our lives than our relationship with God. Jesus says, "No one can serve two masters . . . . You cannot serve God and wealth" (Matt. 6:24). The same can be said for sports: One cannot serve God and sports. When a commitment from sports prevents one from being able to make a commitment to a faith community or when one's obsession with a game keeps one from being fully present with others or when one is willing to spend hundreds of dollars on tickets to a game but not to spend a greater amount on those who are poor and hungry and sick, he or she has placed sports ahead of God's priorities.

My intent is not to be critical. I have confessed that I am sometimes guilty of making sports into an idol. Truly putting God first and focusing on God's priorities can be difficult. Jesus said, "If any want to become my followers, let them deny themselves and take up their cross and follow me" (Mark 8:34), implying that a life of Christian discipleship requires extraordinary sacrifice. While we need not sacrifice sports to faithfully follow Christ, we do need to be mindful of our attitude and approach to sports. We need to make sure that sports enhance our relationships with others instead of interfering with them. We should participate in sports in ways that are beneficial to our health, not in ways that cause us anxiety or burnout. And, most importantly, we must allow sports to point us to God instead of allowing sports to distract us from God.

EPILOGUE

Glimpses of God

Only four kinds of events—politics, religion,
the arts, and sports—have been able to draw consistently
large crowds of paying customers throughout history.
That must mean something.

—BILL RUSSELL

For as I went through the city and looked carefully
at the objects of your worship, I found among them an alter with
the inscription, "To an unknown god." What therefore you
worship as unknown, this I proclaim to you.

—ACTS 17:23

When the Apostle Paul traveled to Athens he was "deeply distressed to see that the city was full of idols" (Acts 17:16). But when he stood on the Areopagus to preach, he didn't deliver a sermon of judgment or condemnation; instead he made connections between the Athenians' culture and religion—including their idolatry—and his message of new life in Christ. He specifically named an idol that bore the inscription,

"To an unknown God" (17:23), and suggested that this "unknown" God was none other than the God who had been manifest in Christ, "[t]he God who made the world and everything in it" (17:24). Quoting Greek poets familiar to his audience, Paul explained, "In [God] we live and move and have our being. . . For we too are his offspring" (17:28). Paul showed the Athenians how their religion and culture pointed to a greater reality and how their idols gave them a glimpse of a living God who was truly worthy of their worship and devotion.

This book follows the example that Paul set in Athens. As we saw in the last chapter, sports are, for many, an object of devotion and worship. Fans order their lives around when their favorite teams play; many athletes—some of whom are very young—devote so much time and energy to their sport that other aspects of their lives suffer. Paul acknowledged that the Athenians had a very rich culture but understood that their idols were not worthy objects of worship. Instead, he saw their culture as a window that looked out upon a greater reality and gave them a glimpse of a God who was worthy of their devotion. This book has explored much of what is truly good about sports, while making clear that sports should not be an object of worship. It has described several glimpses of God that fans and players may have experienced while watching or participating in the games they love so much: the persistent hope of Chicago Cubs fans, the perseverance and tenacity of Daniel "Rudy" Reuttiger, the courage of Jackie Robinson and Roberto Clemente, the miracle performed by the United States hockey team in the 1980 Olympics, and the pregame rituals that give a team a sense of unity and purpose.

My hope is that those readers who identify themselves both as sports fans and disciples of Christ will be able to see God at work in the sports they enjoy. When you see a team of underdogs pull together to beat the odds and accomplish great things, you get a taste of what God desires and expects from the church. When you see a simple ritual give a group of athletes a sense of purpose and identification with something larger than themselves, you get a sense of how one can experience God's grace through ritual and tradition. When you witness a seemingly miraculous last-second, game-winning play, you remember that, through God, all things are possible. When you spend time with your family telling stories of the big games you've seen and the great players you've watched, you should consider how much more important it is to tell God's story of creation and redemption.

As you play, watch, and read about sports, pay attention to the ways in which God is present on the field, court, or track or in the pool. Be mindful of what God may be teaching you through the sports you play and/or love. Sports need not compete with our faith for our attention and devotion. Instead, we can claim sports as one more way in which God speaks to us today.

Appendix A

College Programs and National Championships
by Religious Affiliation

DIVISION I COLLEGE ATHLETIC PROGRAMS BY SCHOOL RELIGIOUS AFFILIATION

Roman Catholic

Boston College

Canisius College

College of the Holy Cross

Fordham University

Georgetown University

Gonzaga University

Iona College

La Salle University

Loyola College in Maryland

Loyola Marymount University

Loyola University Chicago

Marist College

Marquette University

Mount St. Mary's University

Sacred Heart University

Santa Clara University

Seton Hall University

Siena College

St. John's University

St. Joseph's University

St. Francis College

St. Francis University

St. Mary's College of California

St. Peter's College

University of Detroit Mercy

University of Notre Dame

University of San Diego

University of San Francisco

Villanova University

Xavier University

United Methodist

American University

Bethune-Cookman University

Boston University

Centenary College of Louisiana

Duke University

High Point University

Southern Methodist University

Syracuse University

University of Denver

University of Evansville

University of the Pacific

Wofford College

Baptist

Baylor University

Belmont University

Campbell University

Charleston Southern University

Houston Baptist University

Liberty University

Samford University

Wake Forest University

Presbyterian

Davidson University
Presbyterian College
University of Tulsa

Lutheran (Evangelical Lutheran Church of America)

Wagner University

Lutheran (Missouri Synod)

Valparaiso University

Church of Christ

David Lipscomb University
Pepperdine University

Christian Church (Disciples of Christ)

Texas Christian University

United Church of Christ

Elon University

Charismatic

Oral Roberts University

Latter-Day Saints

Brigham Young University

NCAA MEN'S DIVISION I BASKETBALL CHAMPIONS BY RELIGIOUS AFFILIATION

Roman Catholic (8)

College of the Holy Cross (1947)
La Salle University (1954)
University of San Francisco (1955, 1956)
Loyola University of Chicago (1963)
Marquette University (1977)
Georgetown University (1984)
Villanova University (1985)

United Methodist (4)

Duke University (1991, 1992, 2001)
Syracuse University (2003)

NCAA WOMEN'S DIVISION I BASKETBALL CHAMPIONS BY RELIGIOUS AFFILIATION

Baptist (1)

Baylor University (2005)

AIAW WOMEN'S DIVISION I BASKETBALL CHAMPIONS BY RELIGIOUS AFFILIATION

(Prior to 1982, the NCAA did not oversee women's sports. The highest level of collegiate competition in women's basketball was under the administration of the Association for Intercollegiate Athletics for Women [AIAW].)

Roman Catholic (3)

Immaculata University (1972, 1973, 1974)

NCAA DIVISION IA/FBS FOOTBALL CHAMPIONS BY RELIGIOUS AFFILIATION

(Several organizations award college football national championships. A handful—such as those awarded by the Associated Press, *USA Today*, United Press International, and the recent Bowl Championship Series—are recognized as consensus national championships. Others are not, but nonetheless recognize teams that can make a legitimate case for being the nation's best. Below, nonconsensus national championships are denoted by an asterisk.)

Roman Catholic

University of Notre Dame (1919, 1920*, 1924, 1927, 1929, 1930, 1938*, 1943, 1946, 1947, 1949, 1953*, 1964, 1966, 1967*, 1970*, 1973, 1977, 1988, 1989*, 1993*)
University of Detroit Mercy (1928*)

United Methodist

Southern Methodist University (1935*, 1981*, 1982*)
Syracuse University (1959)

Disciples of Christ

Texas Christian University (1935*, 1938)

Latter-Day Saints

Brigham Young University (1983)

Presbyterian

Centre College (1919*)

Appendix B
Religiously Inspired Sports Nicknames and Terminology

SPORTS TEAMS WITH RELIGIOUSLY THEMED NICKNAMES

Major League Baseball

Los Angeles Angels of Anaheim
San Diego Padres

National Football League

New Orleans Saints

National Hockey League

New Jersey Devils

NCAA Division I

DePaul Blue Demons
Duke Blue Devils
Holy Cross Crusaders
Pennsylvania Quakers
Providence Friars
Siena Saints
Valparaiso Crusaders
Wake Forest Demon Deacons

A GLOSSARY OF RELIGIOUSLY INSPIRED SPORTS TERMINOLOGY

Cathedral of Rugby: A nickname for Loftus Versfeld Stadium in Pretoria, South Africa.

Control their own destiny: Not a reference to free will, but to a team's ability to win a conference, division, or playoff spot without having to rely on other teams losing.

David: The legendary king of Israel who was anointed as the successor to King Saul when he was still a young boy (1 Sam. 16:1–13). Soon thereafter, while delivering food to his older brothers on the front lines of battle, David responded to a challenge issued by Goliath, a giant warrior representing Israel's neighbor and enemy, Philistia. David, though small in stature and unarmed aside from a sling and some stones, defeated the giant (1 Sam. 17:1–51). Among sportscasters, David has become a metaphor for underdogs who exceed expectations and defeat more talented and esteemed opponents. (See also "Goliath.")

Deacon: A church leader whose responsibilities involve service and who, in many traditions, lacks the authority of a priest, elder, or bishop. "Deacon" was a nickname for baseball players Bill McKechnie and Vern Law because of the players' active participation in their respective churches. It is also more famously the nickname of Pro Football Hall of Fame defensive end David "Deacon" Jones, but for Jones the nickname likely had no religious significance.

Father Marriott: The nickname of early twentieth-century English cricket bowler Charles Marriott. "Father" alluded to another Charles Marriott who had been a well-known Anglican priest in the nineteenth century.

Goliath: The name of a Philistine giant who was so intimidating that none of the soldiers in the Israelite army had the courage to face him. The giant talked a lot of trash but was ultimately defeated by David, a young shepherd boy who took him down with a sling and a stone. Sports broadcasters often use Goliath to describe heavily favored teams and athletes who surprisingly lose to less celebrated opponents. (See also "David.")

Hail Mary: A long forward pass in football attempted in the waning moments of a game or half that has little chance of being completed. The name of the play alludes to the Roman Catholic prayer ritual in which one asks the Virgin Mary to intercede on one's behalf. The phrase was first used as a football term to describe the play that the Dallas Cowboys used to defeat the Minnesota Vikings in the 1975 NFC Championship Game. Quarterback Roger Staubach, who completed the desperation pass to wide receiver Drew Pearson, told the Pro Football Hall of Fame in 2000, "It was 14–10 at the time and time was running out. When I threw the ball to Pearson, I kind of under-threw it. The term 'Hail Mary' was developed because after the game, I told the press I closed my eyes and said a 'Hail Mary.'"[1]

Other famous Hail Mary passes include the Minnesota Vikings' Tommy Kramer's last-second pass to Ahmad Rashad to beat the Cleveland Browns during the 1980 NFL season; Doug Flutie's desperation bomb in the final seconds of Boston College's 1984 victory over Miami; and Kordell Stewart of the University of Colorado flinging a sixty-four-yard touchdown pass on the final play of a 1994 game against Michigan.

Holy Cow: An exclamation first used by baseball broadcaster Halsey Hall,[2] who did games for the minor league Minneapolis Millers, and popularized by Yankees player and broadcaster Phil Rizzuto and Harry Carey, broadcaster for the St. Louis Cardinals, Chicago White Sox, and (most famously) Chicago Cubs. Some have made connections between the phrase and the sanctity of the bovine in the Hindu tradition. It is more likely an allusion to the golden calf in Exodus 32 or a way of saying "Holy Christ" without using the Lord's name in vain.

Holy War: The nickname of the annual college football game between in-state rivals Brigham Young University and the University of Utah. The moniker also applies to games between Boston College and the University of Notre Dame, the only Roman Catholic schools in college football's highest classification.

Immaculate Reception: The famous and controversial play that gave the Pittsburgh Steelers a lead (and ultimately a victory) over the Oakland Raiders in the final seconds of a 1972 AFC playoff game. With less than thirty seconds remaining and trailing the Raiders 7–6, the Steelers faced a fourth down at their own forty-yard line. Scrambling and under pressure, quarterback Terry Bradshaw threw a long pass to receiver Frenchy Fuqua. Raiders defender Jack Tatum arrived just in time to keep Fuqua from making the catch. The ball bounced off of Tatum and/or Fuqua and into the hands of Steelers running back Franco Harris, who ran the ball into the end zone for the winning touchdown.[3]

The ruling on the field was that the ball bounced off of Tatum without touching Fuqua, earning the play the nickname "Immaculate Reception," a play on "Immaculate Conception," the Roman Catholic dogma that says that the Virgin Mary was conceived without the stain of original sin. Had the ball touched Fuqua—and some maintain that it did—the play would have been illegal. At the time two offensive players were not allowed to touch a pass in succession.

Minister of Defense: A nickname for late NFL hall-of-famer Reggie White (of the Philadelphia Eagles, Green Bay Packers, and Carolina Panthers), who was both one of the greatest defensive players in pro football history and an ordained Baptist preacher. White recalls the beginning of his ministerial career in his 1996 autobiography *In the Trenches*: "When I was seventeen years old, I went before a group of ministers at St. John's Baptist Church in Chattanooga and gave a trial sermon on the subject of forgiveness. . . . I don't think the ministers judging my sermon saw any heavenly lights. But at least they thought I'd done a passable job, and they gave me my minister's license."[4] Later, when describing the Eagles defense in the late 1980s, White says, "Me? I was the Minister of Defense, the Rev. It was my job to put the fear of God into the guys on the other side of the line."[5]

Miracle: An extraordinary event often thought to be supernatural. Sportscasters and fans often use the word "miracle" to describe an incredible play or an unlikely outcome to a game. Perhaps the most famous sporting miracle was the Miracle on Ice, the United States hockey team's upset over the heavily favored Soviets in the 1980 Lake Placid Olympics. More recently, the Tennessee Titans' last-second, game-winning kickoff return against the Buffalo Bills in the 1999–2000 NFL Playoffs was dubbed the Music City Miracle. See chapter 9 for more on these and other miracles.

Prayer: A petition for divine intervention, as in "He threw up a prayer." "Prayer" is often used by sportscasters to describe a last-second shot in a basketball or a desperation pass in a football game (possibly on a fourth down or long third down or in the waning moments of a half).

Promised Land: A championship. The phrase often is used when talking about a promising free agent or draft pick who may have the potential to lead a team to the "Promised Land." (For instance, "Kevin Garnett may be the right player to lead the Celtics to the Promised

Land.") In scripture, the promised land was the land of Canaan, where Abraham had lived. When the people of Israel, who were Abraham's descendants, were slaves in Egypt, God promised to deliver them from captivity and take them back to the land of their ancestors.

God selected Moses (an Israelite who had been raised as an Egyptian but who was on the run after murdering an Egyptian slave master) to lead Israel to freedom. Thus players who take their teams to the "Promised Land" are sometimes compared to Moses. But Moses never actually made it to Canaan. He died atop Mount Nebo in Moab from where he could see the land God had promised his people (Deut. 32:48–52). In the 1996 movie *Soul of the Game*, about the Negro Leagues and Jackie Robinson breaking baseball's "color barrier," the Satchel Paige character (played by Delroy Lindo) imagines the day when African American ball players can play in the majors and worries that he might be like Moses— that his career would end before his people got to the "Promised Land."[6] (Paige ended up playing five seasons in the majors.)

Steeplechase: A form of horse racing that involves jumping fences, running through ditches, and navigating other obstacles and a middle-distance track-and-field event involving hurdles and water traps. The sport's name comes from the church steeples used for the orientation of early race courses.

Touchdown Jesus: A large mural of the risen Christ on the side of Notre Dame University's Hesburgh Library that overlooks the school's football stadium. In the mural, Jesus's raised arms resemble those of a referee signaling a touchdown.

Appendix C
A Dictionary of Inspirational Sports Movies

Breaking Away (20th Century Fox, 1979): A group of four aimless recent high school graduates in Bloomington, Indiana, get an opportunity to enter a team in Indiana University's Little 500 bicycle race. They call their team the "Cutters," a derogatory name for Bloomington residents who are not affiliated with the university, several of whom work in the nearby limestone quarries. One character, Dave, is obsessed with Italian culture and European cycling and leads the Cutters to victory. Nominated for the Academy Award for Best Picture.

Brian's Song (Columbia Pictures, 1971): Based on the true story of Chicago Bears teammates Brian Piccolo and Gale Sayers as told in Sayers's autobiography *I Am Third*. The two players become close friends despite competing for the Bears' starting running back position. Their friendship grows closer when Piccolo is diagnosed with cancer.

Coach Carter (Paramount, 2005): Based on the true story of a California high school basketball coach who benched his undefeated team when several players' grades slipped. The community protests Coach Carter's decision, but his players buy in and agree not to play until they improve their grades. Eventually the team returns to the court and takes its good grades all the way to the state championship game.

Chariots of Fire (Warner Bros., 1981): Perhaps best known for its iconic, synthesizer-driven soundtrack, *Chariots* tells the true story of British runners Harold Abrahams and Eric Liddell at the 1924 Olympic Games. Liddell, because of his Christian faith, refuses to run in the 100-meter race, which is held on a Sunday. But teammate Andrew Lindsay offers to take Liddell's place in the 100 and allows Liddell to take Lindsay's place in the 400. Liddell wins the 400; meanwhile Abrahams, who is Jewish, overcomes anti-Semitism to win the 100. Winner of the Academy Award for Best Picture.

Cool Runnings (Walt Disney Pictures, 1993): A comedic take on the true story of the first Jamaican bobsled team. Under the tutelage of a disgraced former bobsledder from the United States, a team of three Jamaican sprinters and a pushcart driver qualify for the 1988 Winter Olympics in Calgary, Alberta.

Glory Road (Walt Disney Pictures, 2006): Based on the true story of the 1966 Texas Western basketball team—the first team with an all–African American starting lineup to win an NCAA basketball championship. The team faces a heavily favored, all-white Kentucky team in the title game.

The Greatest Game Ever Played (Buena Vista Pictures, 2005): Based on the true story of Francis Ouimet, an unheralded amateur golfer who surprised onlookers by defeating the best golfers in the world and winning the 1913 U.S. Open.

Hoosiers (Orion Pictures, 1986): A former college coach with a checkered past leads an undermanned basketball team from a small, rural Indiana high school to a state championship in the early 1950s. The story is very loosely based on the story of the team from tiny Milan High School that won the state title over heavily favored powerhouse Muncie Central in 1954.

A League of Their Own (Columbia Pictures, 1992): During World War II, when several ball players are overseas serving in the military, a wealthy businessman starts a women's professional baseball league. The league struggles at first but gains popularity as the public gets a taste of the abilities and personalities of the players. The plot is roughly based on the true story of the All-American Girls Professional Baseball League.

Miracle (Walt Disney Pictures, 2004): Based on the true story of the United States hockey team's improbable gold medal performance at the 1980 Winter Olympics. An American team of unknown college players and amateurs meets a heavily favored Soviet team in the medal round and shocks the world by winning 4–3. The team goes on to defeat Finland and win the gold.

Our Lady of Victory (2009): Based on the true story of the Immaculata Mighty Macs. A young and inexperienced coach leads the basketball team at a small, Roman Catholic, all-women's college near Philadelphia to three national championships in the early 1970s.

The Pride of the Yankees (RKO Radio Pictures, 1942): The true story of Yankees great Lou Gehrig, whose career is cut short by a battle with amyotrophic lateral sclerosis, a disease that would come to be known as Lou Gehrig's disease.

Remember the Titans (Walt Disney Pictures, 2000): Based on a true story. The success of a state championship football team heals racial divisions at a recently integrated Virginia high school.

Rocky (United Artists, 1976): A small-time Philadelphia club fighter gets a shot at undefeated heavyweight champion Apollo Creed. Winner of the Academy Award for Best Picture.

Rudy (TriStar Pictures, 1993): Based on the true story of Daniel "Rudy" Reuttiger, who, despite being undersized for a college football player and struggling from dyslexia, was accepted to Notre Dame and was able to walk on to the football team. Thanks to the sacrifices of his teammates Rudy gets an opportunity to play in the final series of the final game of his senior season.

Seabiscuit (Universal Pictures, 2003): Based on a true story and Laura Hillenbrand's book *Seabiscuit: An American Legend*. During the Great Depression an undersized and unheralded race horse comes from nowhere to become the best race horse in the world and a symbol of hope for Depression-era America. Nominated for the Academy Award for Best Picture.

Soul of the Game (Home Box Office, 1996): Tells the true story of integration in baseball. Soul of the Game follows Negro League players Jackie Robinson, Satchel Paige, and Josh Gibson leading up to Robinson's major league debut with the Brooklyn Dodgers.

We Are Marshall (Warner Bros., 2006): Based on a true story. After most of the football players and coaches at Marshall University die in a 1970 plane crash, the school's administration considers discontinuing the football program. But at the urging of the student body, the school hires a new coach to rebuild the team. Over the course of a difficult season, the team of freshmen, walk-ons, and the few survivors from the previous year's team learns to hold its own on the football field.

Appendix D
Answer Key for the Hypothetical Water-Cooler
Conversations on Page xxx (Chapter 10)

1. Eighth-seeded Villanova upsets top-ranked and heavily favored Georgetown to win the 1985 Men's NCAA Basketball Championship.

2. An injured Kirk Gibson hobbles to the plate to hit a game-winning home run for the Dodgers in his only at bat in the 1988 World Series.

3. Nadia Comaneci becomes the first gymnast in modern Olympic history to score a 10. In all, Comaneci would get seven perfect 10s and win three gold medals, one silver medal, and one bronze medal in the 1976 Olympics in Montreal.[1]

4. Greg LeMond comes from behind in the final stage of the 1989 Tour de France to defeat Laurent Fignon by only eight seconds, the closest margin in history.

5. The basketball team at Immaculata, a small all-women's college outside of Philadelphia, wins three consecutive AIAW championships in the early 1970s.

6. Kurt Warner comes from nowhere to earn a spot as a back up quarterback for the St. Louis Rams. He takes over for injured starter Trent Green and leads the Rams to a Super Bowl victory.

7. The United States hockey team upsets the heavily favored Soviets in the 1980 Olympics in Lake Placid, New York.

Notes

INTRODUCTION

1. Rollen Stewart's story is the subject of Sam Green's independently released 1997 documentary *Rainbow Man/John 3:16*.

2. See "Kurt Warner on Love, Life, and God," CBN.com, http://www.cbn .com/entertainment/sports/kurtwarner_2002.aspx, accessed November 2008.

3. I attended the University of Evansville. Our fight song, "Hail to Evansville," contains the lyric "Cheering with pep and vim for white and purple."

4. Bill Russell and Taylor Branch, *Second Wind: The Memoirs of an Opinionated Man* (New York: Random House, 1979).

CHAPTER 1: "LIFE BEGINS ON OPENING DAY"

1. Randy Horick, "Commentary: Remembering One Woman's Faith, Battle With ALS," The United Methodist News Service (June 19, 2006), http://www.umc.org/site/c.gjTJbMUIuE/b.1800809/k.4BF2/Commentary_ Remembering_one_womans_faith_battle_with_ALS.htm.

2. Ibid.

3. Ibid.

4. The 1975 series featured Carlton Fisk's famous walk-off home run in Game 6—the game-winning dinger that Fisk memorably "waved fair."

5. Instead of directing their anger toward Boone, many Sox fans focused instead on Boston manger Grady Little, who opted to keep pitching ace Pedro Martinez in the game into the eighth inning. The Sox had a 5-2 lead going into the eighth, but Martinez pitched one inning too many and the lead quickly evaporated. The team fired Little following the 2003 season.

6. Related reading: Josh Tinley, "Perseverance and the Cubs," Abingdon Youth.com, http://www.ileadyouth.com/article_reader.asp?ID=246. I wrote this article during the Cubs' 2003 playoff run.

7. Josh Tinley, "Five Things the Titans Need to Do," Josh Tinley.com (September 18, 2006), http://scrambies.blogspot.com/2006/09/five-things-ti-tans-need-to-do.html.

8. Ibid. Concerning Coach Fisher, I wrote: "I love Jeff Fisher and think he's an excellent coach, but the Titans need a sea change right now; not only has the team become a mainstay in the NFL's lower echelon, but they are also showing little promise for the future. Sure, the Titans have some promising young players, but these players are being formed by a culture of losing, resignation, and futility. A new face on the sidelines might be a necessary first step toward transformation."

9. Northwestern lost in the Rose Bowl to the University of Southern California 41–32, blemishing their previously perfect bowl record.

10. This metaphor has its limits. While sports leagues begin new seasons each year indefinitely, a person can only be baptized once. For ancient Christians, baptism acted as a seal, protecting the convert from sin. This understanding of the sacrament caused problems as baptized Christians continued to sin. During the Decian persecution of the third century, for instance, many Christians followed the emperor's orders to make sacrifices to the Roman gods. Although their lives were spared, these members of the church were guilty of apostasy. The death of Decius and the end of the persecution was the beginning of a heated debate among church leaders regarding the fate of these baptized apostates. See W. H. C. Frend, *The Rise of Christianity* (Minneapolis: Fortress Press, 1984), 141, 318–25.)

11. The Articles of Religion of the Methodist Church were adopted by The United Methodist Church following the union of the Methodist and Evangelical United Brethren Churches in 1968.

12. From *The Book of Discipline of The United Methodist Church 2004* (Nashville: United Methodist Publishing House, 2005), 103, p. 63.

CHAPTER 2: THE LAST WILL BE FIRST

1. Scholars question whether David actually fought Goliath. According to 2 Samuel 21:19, Elhanan son of Jaareoregim was responsible for slaying Goliath the Gittite. Notice also that, throughout much of the David-Goliath story, David's adversary is referred to as "the Philistine." An editor may have attached Goliath's name and legend to the story of an anonymous Philistine champion whom David killed.

2. Stephen Prothero, *Religious Literacy* (Harper SanFrancisco, 2007), 173.

3. Details about these facilities can be found on the University of Kentucky's website, http://www.uky.edu/EVPFA/Facilities/CPMD/Capital Projects/currentconstruction/bpf/bpf.htm.

4. Larry Schwartz, "Billie Jean won for all women," *ESPN.com*, http://espn .go.com/sportscentury/features/00016060.html.

5. Rudy's height and weight were 5'6" and 165 when he played for Notre Dame according to his official website; see http://www.rudyinternational .com/truestory1.cfm.

6. *Rudy*, David Anspaugh, director (Tri-Star Pictures, 1993), motion picture.

7. Exodus 16. The Israelites approach Moses and Aaron, angry that their food supply is running out and the promised land is nowhere in sight. God mercifully responds by sending manna from heaven. The people are only allowed to take exactly what they need: "when they measured it with an omer, those who gathered much had nothing over, and those who gathered little had

no shortage; they gathered as much as each of them needed" (verse 18). They also were not allowed to store any of the food to save it for later: "Some left part of it until morning, and it bred worms and became foul" (verse 20).

8. Exodus 32. The Israelites grow impatient with Moses and demand that Aaron, the people's priestly leader, make them "gods." The result is an idol in the image of a calf, crafted from all the gold articles in the Israelites' possession.

9. Numbers 13–14. Israelite spies are sent into Canaan to scout the land that God has promised to the people of Israel. The spies report that the Anak—a race of giants descended from the Nephilim (see Gen. 6:1-4)—occupy the land, and the Israelites nearly unanimously say that they will not enter the land to which God is leading them. Only Moses, Aaron, and two of the spies—Joshua and Canaan—have the courage to faithfully obey God's instructions. God threatens to wipe out the faithless people, but Moses intervenes and God relents. Still, God will not allow any of the current generation of Israelites, aside from Joshua and Caleb, to enter the promised land.

10. Numbers 20:8–18. Again the Israelites are not satisfied with the state of affairs; this time, they're concerned about their lack of water for cleaning and drinking. God mercifully enables Moses and Aaron to draw water from a rock. Here, God punishes Moses and Aaron for their inability or reluctance (the text isn't entirely clear) to "show [God's] holiness before the eyes of the Israelites" (verse 12).

CHAPTER 3: NEITHER JEW NOR GREEK, SLAVE NOR FREE

1. As of this writing, Duke's men's basketball program has retired thirteen of the thirty-six eligible college basketball uniform numbers.

2. See Jackie Robinson and Alfred Duckett, *I Never Had It Made* (New York: Harper Collins, 1995; first edition Putnam, 1972), 32–33.

3. Ibid., xxii–xxiii.

4. Ibid., 27.

5. Ibid., 61.

6. Bernardo Ruiz, director, *American Experience: Roberto Clemente* (PBS 2008), DVD.

7. Ibid.

8. Ibid.

9. Although the leagues were distinct, major league teams and Negro league teams were known to compete against each other in unofficial exhibition games.

10. Some would add that, because of expansion, today's greats are also putting up numbers against a diluted talent pool. One could counter that argument by noting that improved youth, high school, and college programs, along with an influx of world-class Latin American and Asian players, have led to an increase in major-league-caliber talent.

11. Dan Klores, director, *Black Magic* (ESPN Films 2008), DVD.

12. Maya Angelou, *I Know Why the Caged Bird Sings* (New York, Bantam, 1971), 114.

13. Ibid., 115.

14. See Jeremy Schaap, *Triumph: The Untold Story of Jesse Owens and Hitler's Olympics* (Boston: Houghton Mifflin, 2007), 34, http://books.google.com /books?id=DSsdGalGcPMC&printsec=frontcover&dq=triumph#PPA34,M1 ; Doug Gillon, "Jesse Owens: Olympic Icon," *The Herald* (February 16, 2009), http://www.theherald.co.uk/sport/thearchive/display.var.2489453.0.jesse_owens _olympic_icon.php.

15. "Jesse Owens," CNN.com (July 7, 2008), http://edition.cnn.com/2008 /SPORT/05/01/jesseowens/index.html.

16. "Biography," http://www.jesseowens.com/about/.

17. Klores, *Black Magic*.

18. Ibid.

19. "March Madness Flashback: John Wooden," *ISU News* (March 30, 2006).

20. See "History of the NAIA," NAIA.org, http://naia.cstv.com/genrel /090905aai.html.

21. Richard Lapchick, "Althea Gibson Must Be Smiling over Venus, Serena," ESPN.com (July 9, 2008), http://sports.espn.go.com/sports/tennis /columns/story?columnist=lapchick_richard&id=3478200.

22. SportsPickle.com, a sports satire website, took on this subject in an article titled "Mixed Race Athlete Said to Be Both Scrappy AND Athletic," http://www.sportspickle.com/features/volume7/2008-0402-race.html.

23. ESPN's Stephen A. Smith, who is outspoken on the subject of race and sports, said as much in this May 19, 2008, *ESPN, the Magazine* column, "So the NBA Is Getting Whiter? I've Got No Problem with That," http://sports .espn.go.com/espnmag/story?id=3382363.

24. Amy-Jill Levine, *The Misunderstood Jew* (San Francisco: Harper-SanFrancisco, 2006), 69.

25. From a 1963 speech at Western Michigan University. See Western Michigan's Archives and Regional Histories Collection at http://www.wmich .edu/library/archives/mlk/q-a.html.

26. See "A Survey of United Methodist Laity and Clergy: The Connectional Table" (October 23, 2006), http://www.umc.org/atf/cf/% 7BDB6A45E4-C446-4248-82C8-E131B6424741%7D/CTQuantitative Final.pdf.

CHAPTER 4: "EQUAL WORTH IN THE EYES OF GOD"

1. "The Nurturing Community: Women and Men," The Social Principles of The United Methodist Church; from The Book of Discipline of The

United Methodist Church 2004 (Nashville, TN: The United Methodist Publishing House 2004), ¶ 161

2. "Athletics," TitleIX.info, http://www.titleix.info/10-Key-Areas-of-Title-IX/Athletics.aspx.

3. Ibid.

4. Cokie Roberts, "Interview with Billie Jean King," *USA Weekend* (April 6, 2008), http://www.usaweekend.com/08_issues/080406/080406billie-jean-king.html.

5. Aditi Kinkhabwala, "Sex Sells? Not So Fast," *Sports Illustrated* (May 9, 2007), http://sportsillustrated.cnn.com/2007/writers/aditi_kinkhabwala/05/09/better.half/index.html.

6. Ibid.

7. I wrote about this on my blog. See Josh Tinley, " SI Wipes the Specks Out of America's Eyes, Ignores the Log in Its Own," Josh Tinley.com (May 10, 2007), http://scrambies.blogspot.com/2007/05/si-wipes-specks-out-of-americas-eyes.html.

8. Darren Rovell, "Will She or Won't She? Playboy Still Waiting," ESPN.com Page 2 (July 24, 2001), http://espn.go.com/page2/s/rovell/010724.html.

9. "Worlds Sexiest Athletes: Lisa Harrison," ESPN.com, http://espn.go.com/sexiestathletes/lisa_harrison.html.

10. Josh Tinley, "CNN Sends Curious Message to Girls Who Are Interested in Football," Josh Tinley.com (October 09, 2008), http://scrambies.blogspot.com/2008/10/cnn-sends-curious-message-to-girls-who.html.

11. David Carr, "Networks condemn remarks by Imus," *New York Times* (April 7, 2007), http://www.nytimes.com/2007/04/07/arts/television/07imus.html?_r=1&hp.

12. "The Nurturing Community: Women and Men," *The Social Principles of The United Methodist Church; from The Book of Discipline of The United Methodist Church 2004* (Nashville: United Methodist Publishing House, 2004), par. 161.

13. "The Social Community: Rights of Women," *The Social Principles of The United Methodist Church; from The Book of Discipline of The United Methodist Church 2004* (Nashville: United Methodist Publishing House, 2004), par 162.

14. Ibid.

CHAPTER 5: ONE BODY, MANY PARTS

1. Bernie Schneider, "1953–56 NCAA Championship Seasons: The Bill Russell Years," USFDons.com, http://usfdons.cstv.com/trads/russell_years.html.

2. Bill Russell and Taylor Branch, *Second Wind* (New York: Random House, 1979), 121.

3. Ibid., 124.

4. See "Hall of Famers by Position," The Official Site of the Pro Football Hall of Fame, http://www.profootballhof.com/hof/positions.html. Jan Stenerud is the only "pure" placekicker in the Hall of Fame. Three other placekickers are in the Hall of Fame, but all three were inducted largely for their performance at other positions. George Blanda was primarily a quarterback; Paul Hornung was mainly a halfback; and Lou Groza played most of his snaps on the offensive line. Yale Lary, in the Hall of Fame as a defensive back, doubled as a punter.

5. Fans of the Buffalo Bills will not soon forget Scott Norwood missing a potential game-winning kick in the final seconds of Super Bowl XXV. On the other hand, Bostonians will long remember Adam Vinatieri's late placekicking heroics in all three of the New England Patriots' Super Bowl victories. See Tom Pedulla, "In the playoffs, it's the little things that make differences," *USA Today* (January 5, 2006), http://www.usatoday.com/sports/football/nfl/2006-01-05-bonus-mainbar_x.htm.

CHAPTER 6: TOUCHING THE ROCK

1. I want to give credit where credit is due: my Perry Meridian High School swim team stole the "Go Bananas" ritual from North Central High School, also in Indianapolis.

2. Bernard Murray, "Athletes and Pre-Game Rituals," *The Hilltop Online*, October 10, 2003, http://media.www.thehilltoponline.com/media/storage/paper590/news/2003/10/10/Sports/Athletes.And.PreGame.Rituals-525063.shtml.

3. Ibid.

4. See Mark Rich, "Creatures of Habit," Bulls.com (August 15, 2003), http://www.nba.com/bulls/news/habits_030815.html.

5. Chris Ballard, "One Last Shot for Reggie," *Sports Illustrated*, 102, no. 16 (April 18, 2005), http://vault.sportsillustrated.cnn.com/vault/article/magazine/MAG1110780/2/index.htm.

6. Ibid.

7. Boggs played out his final seasons with the Tampa Bay Devil Rays (who have since dropped the "Devil" and are now just the "Rays").

8. Carter Gaddis, "A Boggs Life," Tampa Bay Online (August 8, 1999), http://tampabayonline.net/rays/wade3000/rutine.htm.

9. For more on interesting athlete superstitions, see Jason Murdoch, "Superstitious Athletes," CBC Sports Online Top 10 (May 10, 2005), http://www.cbc.ca/sports/columns/top10/superstition.html.

10. Kenda Creasy Dean and Ron Foster, *The Godbearing Life* (Nashville: Upper Room Books, 1998), 112.

11. Ibid.

12. Scott Taylor, "Brouhaha Haka: Pregame Ritual—Which BYU Does—Is Still under Spotlight," *Deseret Morning News*, September 13, 2007, http://deseretnews.com/article/1,5143,695209541,00.html.

13. "Cathy Rush's 2008 Hall of Fame Induction Speech," NBA TV (September 6, 2008), web video, http://broadband.nba.com/cc/playa.php ?content=video&url=http://boss.streamos.com/wmedia/nba/nbacom/hof/hof _speech_rush.asx&video=blank.

14. Mark Schlabach, "Gift from Death Valley Became 'Death Valley' Tradition," ESPN.com (September 14, 2007), http://sports.espn.go.com/ncf /columns/story?columnist=schlabach_mark&id=3017840.

15. Ibid.

16. Ibid.

17. See Travis Measley, "Texas A&M Has Hated Rival Texas to Thank for Some Traditions," ESPN.com (February 3, 2008), http://sports.espn.go.com/ ncb/columns/story?id=3220036.

18. Keith Bradsher, "When Octopuses Are Flying in Detroit It's . . . ," *New York Times* (April 14, 1996), http://query.nytimes.com/gst/fullpage.html ?res=9E00E0DA1139F937A25757C0A960958260.

19. Diana Butler Bass, *Christianity for the Rest of Us: How the Neighborhood Church Is Transforming the Faith* (San Francisco: HarperSanFrancisco, 2006), 172.

20. Marjorie Corbman, *A Tiny Step Away From Deepest Faith* (Brewster, Mass.: Paraclete Press, 2005), 21.

21. William J. Abraham, *Wesley for Armchair Theologians* (Louisville: Westminster John Knox Press, 2005), 114–15.

22. Some have suggested that circumcision—because it applies only to males—is an inherently misogynist ritual and that, by preferring baptism to circumcision, Christians were opting for a more egalitarian initiation ritual. Jewish New Testament scholar Amy-Jill Levine takes issue with this analysis, saying that "there is no evidence that Jewish women felt the need to be circumcised (who could blame them?). Their community considered them full members, and the Jewish literature never refers to them as uncircumcised." She also suggests that baptism is no less patriarchal: "Baptism is a form of 'rebirth' . . . that substitutes the mother's biological role with that of the church." See Amy-Jill Levine, *The Misunderstood Jew* (Harper San Francisco 2006), p. 73.

23. Many scholars agree that Mark, the oldest Gospel, was written in the 60s or early 70s C.E., after most of the Pauline letters.

24. Sandy Weintraub, "Much to Players' Delight, Evansville Leaves Sleeves," *Evansville Courier-Press* (February 13, 2003), http://media.www.dailyorange .com/media/storage/paper522/news/2003/02/13/Sports/Much-To .Players8217.Delight.Evansville.Leaves.Sleeves-368610.shtml.

CHAPTER 7: GYM RATS

1. Since I've begun this chapter, ESPNU, ESPN's network devoted to college athletics, has announced that it will be expanding its coverage of 2008 Midnight Madness celebrations. The network will spend four hours covering Midnight Madness at five schools and peeking in on several others. See "ESPNU to Tip Off College Basketball Season with Expanded Midnight Madness Coverage on Oct. 17," ESPN News Release (October 8, 2008), http://www.espnmediazone.com/press_releases/2008_10_oct/20081008_ESPNUMidnightMadness.htm.

2. David Anspaugh, director, *Hoosiers* (Orion Pictures, 1986), motion picture.

3. "Allen Iverson News Conference Transcript," SI.com (May 10, 2002), http://sportsillustrated.cnn.com/basketball/news/2002/05/09/iverson_transcript/, accessed October 2008.

4. John Papanek, "Gifts That God Didn't Give," *Sports Illustrated* (November 9, 1981), http://sportsillustrated.cnn.com/basketball/nba/1998/bird/flashbacks/1981flash.html.

5. "Happy 50th, Larry Legend," NBA.com, http://www.nba.com/news/birdat50.html.

6. See Mark Levine, "Out There," *The New York Times* (August 3, 2008), http://www.nytimes.com/2008/08/03/sports/playmagazine/803PHELPS-t.html?n=Top/Reference/Times%20Topics/People/P/Phelps, %20Michael& pagewanted=all.

7. H. G. Bissinger, *Friday Night Lights* (Cambridge, Mass.: Da Capo Press, 1990), 25.

8. Permian has struggled since the early 1990s, only advancing to the state finals once and missing the playoffs in several consecutive years.

9. Bissinger, *Friday Night Lights*, 26.

10. Scott Cairns, *A Short Trip to the Edge: Where Earth Meets Heaven—A Pilgrimage* (San Francisco: HarperSanFrancisco, 2007), 30.

11. Ibid, 135.

12. Ibid, 35.

13. "NFL's Passer Rating," Official Site of the Pro Football Hall of Fame, http://www.profootballhof.com/history/release.jsp?release_id=1303.

15. Laura Hillenbrand, *Sea Biscuit: An American Legend* (New York: Ballantine Books, 2001), 82–83.

CHAPTER 8: THE DREADED ASTERISK*

1. Tom Verducci with Don Yaeger, George Dohrmann, Luis Fernando Llosa, and Lester Munson, "Totally Juiced," *Sports Illustrated* (June 3, 2002), http://sportsillustrated.cnn.com/si_online/flashbacks/2002/year_in_review/steroids/.

2. Mark Fainaru-Wada and Lance Williams, "The Truth About Barry Bonds and Steroids," *Sports Illustrated* (February 22, 2006), http://sportsillustrated.cnn.com/2006/magazine/03/06/growth0313/?cnn=yes. This article is an excerpt from Mark Fainaru-Wada and Lance Williams, *Game of Shadows* (New York: Penguin Group, 2006).

3. See Jorge Arangure Jr., "Palmeiro Suspended for Steroid Use," *Washington Post* (August 2, 2005), http://www.washingtonpost.com/wp-dyn/content/article/2005/08/01/AR2005080100739.html.

4. Allen Barra, "The Myth of Maris' Asterisk," Salon.com (October 3, 2001), http://www.salon.com/news/sports/col/barra/2001/10/03/asterisk/.

5. See Mel Antonen, "Ripken, Gwynn Enter Hall of Fame on First Ballot," *USA Today* (January 10, 2007), http://www.usatoday.com/sports/baseball/hallfame/2007-01-09-ripken-gwynn-elected_x.htm.

6. Associated Press, "IOC Strips Jones of All 5 Olympic Medals," NBC Sports (December 12, 2007), http://nbcsports.msnbc.com/id/22170098/.

7. John Clayton, "Gatlin, Banned from Track, Works Out for Texans," ESPN.com (December 1, 2006), http://sports.espn.go.com/nfl/news/story?id=2679967.

8. See Dana O'Neil, "Gray Scale: Recruiters Struggle with Perfectly Legal Yet Ethically Questionable," ESPN.com (November 19, 2008), http://sports.espn.go.com/ncb/columns/story?id=3710807.

9. Ibid.

10. Associated Press, "McCartney 'Remorseful' About Fifth-Down Play," CNNSI.com (June 20, 1998), http://sportsillustrated.cnn.com/football/college/news/1998/06/20/mccartney_fifthdown/.

11. "Hayes Turns Himself in for Using Wrong Ball, DQ'd from PGA Qualifier," ESPN.com (November 23, 2008), http://sports.espn.go.com/golf/news/story?id=3712372.

12. Rick Reilly, "Tired of Athletes and Their Lame Excuses? Kerry Collins Is Your Guy," *ESPN the Magazine* (December 1, 2008), http://sports.espn.go.com/espnmag/story?section=magazine&id=3710467.

CHAPTER 9: FOR SUCH A TIME AS THIS

1. Philip Lee, "Classic Catches Up With Lorenzo Charles," ESPN Classic (November 19, 2003), http://espn.go.com/classic/s/Where_now_charles_lorenzo.html.

2. NC State would be outdone two years later when eighth-seeded Villanova stunned top-ranked and defending champion Georgetown in the 1985 title game.

3. Ahasuerus is generally identified as the Persian king Xerxes I. However, Ahasuerus's wife in Esther, Vashti, is not mentioned in nonbiblical sources. The historian Herodotus names the wife of Xerxes as Amestris.

4. See above.

5. "FCS" stands for "Football Championship Subdivision." For football the NCAA's Division I is split into two subdivisions. The "Football Bowl Subdivision" (FBS), formerly Division I-A, is the highest level of competition and includes most of the nation's most prestigious football programs. Its championship and final rankings are determined by several bowl games. The FCS, formerly Division I-AA, is a slightly lower level of competition and includes smaller programs. The FCS decides its championship through a postseason tournament.

6. For more on Kurt Warner's story see Michael Wilbon, "While the Rams Go Long, Titans Come Up Short," *The Washington Post* (January 30, 2000), http://www.washingtonpost.com/wp-srv/sports/nfl/longterm/1999/super-bowl/stories/wilbon31.htm, and George Vecsey, "Sports of the Times; Kurt Warner Gives Hope to Others," *The New York Times* (February 1, 2000), http://query.nytimes.com/gst/fullpage.html?res=9A0CE3DF173FF932A357 51C0A9669C8B63.

7. Some experts weren't sold on the Rams with or without Green. Glenn Dickey of *Pro Football Weekly* (April 22, 1999), for instance, wrote following the 1999 draft that the hiring of Vermeil had "doomed the Rams to mediocrity beyond the duration for which Vermeil will coach them." Dickey was also critical of the team's selection of Holt in the first round of the draft, calling the pick "boneheaded." See http://archive.profootballweekly.com/content /archives/draft_1998/dickey_042299.asp.

8. Jackie Robinson, *I Never Had It Made* (New York: HarperCollins, 1995), 33.

9. Ibid.

10. See, for example, Vincent M. Mallozzi, "Earl Manigault, 53, New York City Basketball Legend, Dies," *The New York Times* (May 16, 1998), http://query.nytimes.com/gst/fullpage.html?res=9F0DE2DA1130F935A257 56C0A96E958260.

11. See, for example, Dirk Chatelain, "The Mystery of Lawrence Phillips," *Omaha World-Herald* (November 6, 2005), http://www.omaha.com/index .php?u_pg=528&u_xid=13&u_sid=2059729.

12. For more on Josh Hamilton see Albert Chin, "The Super Natural," *Sports Illustrated* (May 27, 2008), http://sportsillustrated.cnn.com/2008/writ-ers/albert_chen/05/27/hamilton0602/.

CHAPTER 10: DO YOU BELIEVE IN MIRACLES?

1. See Rick Weinberg, "18: Cal's Five-Lateral Kickoff Return Shocks Stanford" in "ESPN Counts Down the 100 Most Memorable Moments of the Past 25 Years," ESPN.com, http://sports.espn.go.com/espn/espn25 /story?page=moments/18.

2. While "The Play" did not defy the laws of nature, some critics argue that it defied the rules of college football; many Stanford players and coaches believe strongly that Cal's Dwight Garner was down when he took possession of the ball.

3. Marcus Borg, *The Heart of Christianity* (San Francisco: HarperSanFrancisco, 2003), 155.

4. Ibid., 155–56.

5. See Kevin Allen, "College Kids Perform Olympic Miracle," ESPN Classic (August 11, 2007), reprinted from *USA Hockey: A Celebration of a Great Tradition* (Chicago:Triumph Books, 1997), http://espn.go.com/classic/s/miracle_ice_1980.html.

6. "'Miracle on Ice' Still Unrecognized By Vatican," Left Field Sports, http://leftfieldsports.com/archives/story01_01.htm.

7. Rick Weinberg, "90: Reggie Miller Scores 8 Points in 11 seconds" in "ESPN Counts Down the 100 Most Memorable Moments of the Past 25 Years," ESPN.com, http://sports.espn.go.com/espn/espn25/story?page=moments/90.

CHAPTER 11: "WE COULD ALWAYS TALK ABOUT BASEBALL"

1. As of this writing *Our Lady of Victory* has not yet been released in theaters. A sneak preview of the movie's opening scenes is available at http://www.ourladyofvictorymovie.com/.

2. "AFI's 100 Years, 100 Cheers: America's Most Inspiring Movies" (The American Film Institute, 2005), http://www.afi.com/docs/tvevents/pdf/cheers100.pdf.

3. Associated Press, "Autistic Teen's 20-Point Night Touches All," ESPN.com (February 24, 2006), http://sports.espn.go.com/espn/news/story?id=2343490.

4. Associated Press, "Clemson's McElrathbey Wins Courage Award," ESPN.com (December 14, 2006), http://sports.espn.go.com/ncf/news/story?id=2697195.

5. Sarah Arthur, *The God-Hungry Imagination* (Nashville: Upper Room Books, 2007), 75.

6. Ibid., 82.

7. Daniel Reuttiger is more famously known as "Rudy," mentioned previously.

8. Ron Underwood, director, *City Slickers* (Castle Rock Entertainment, 1991), motion picture.

9. Arthur, *God-Hungry Imagination*, 83.

10. In 1979 only forty teams, rather than the current sixty-five, were selected to play in the NCAA Tournament. So several good teams were relegated to the NIT.

11. Katherine Hankey, "I Love to Tell the Story," ca. 1856.

12. Arthur, *God-Hungry Imagination*, 28.

CHAPTER 12: "TREATED LIKE GODS"

1. "Alou Says He Wouldn't Have Caught Bartman Ball in 2003 NLCS," ESPN.com, http://sports.espn.go.com/mlb/news/story?id=3324343.

2. Ibid.

3. Ibid.

4. "Idol," *The American Heritage® Dictionary of the English Language, Fourth Edition* (Boston: Houghton Mifflin Company, 2004).

5. Walt Mueller, "Turf Worship: When Sports Become a Religion," *Youthworker Journal*, 25, no. 1 (September/October 2008).

6. "Packers Fever Continues," NBC 15.com (January 15, 2008), http://www.nbc15.com/home/headlines/13819247.html.

7. See Jacqueline L. Salmon, "NFL Pulls Plug on Big-Screen Church Parties for Super Bowl," *Washington Post* (February 1, 2008), http://www.washingtonpost.com/wp-dyn/content/article/2008/01/31/AR2008013103958.html. According to the article, "The league bans public exhibitions of its games on TV sets or screens larger than 55 inches because smaller sets limit the audience size."

8. H. G. Bissinger, *Friday Night Lights* (Cambridge, Mass.: Da Capo Press, 1990), 23.

9. Ibid., 24.

10. David Anspaugh, director, *Hoosiers* (Orion Pictures, 1986), motion picture.

11. Bissinger, *Friday Night Lights*, 16.

12. Mike Wise, "Looking Back At Broken 'Dreams,'" *The Washington Post* (July 5, 2004), http://www.washingtonpost.com/ac2/wp-dyn/A27976-2004 Jul4?language=printer.

13. Steve James, director, *Hoop Dreams* (Fine Line Features, 1994), motion picture.

14. Ibid.

15. Wise, "Looking Back."

16. Wise, "Looking Back."

17. Benjy Lipsman, " 'Hoop Dreams' Father Slain," *The Chicagoist*, December 17, 2004, http://chicagoist.com/2004/12/17/hoop_dreams_father_slain.php.

APPENDIX B: Religiously Inspired Sports Nicknames and Terminology

1. "Chat Transcript with Roger Staubach," *Official Site of the Pro Football Hall of Fame* (December 8, 2000), http://www.profootballhof.com/history/release.jsp?release_id=771.

2. "Halsey Hall," The Pavek Museum of Broadcasting, http://www.pavek museum.org/Halsey_Hall.htm.

3. "Two Words Say It All: 'Immaculate Reception,'" ESPN.com (January 8, 1999), http://static.espn.go.com/nfl/playoffs98/news/1999/990106/01030879.html.

4. Reggie White, *In the Trenches* (Nashville: Thomas Nelson, 1996), 39.

5. Ibid., 114.

6. Kevin Rodney Sullivan, *Soul of the Game* (Home Box Office, 1996), made-for-television motion picture.

APPENDIX D: Answer Key for the Hypothetical Water-Coolor Conversations on Page xx (Chapter 10)

1. "Nadia Comaneci," Bart and Nadia.com, http://www.bartandnadia.com/bionadia.html.